DRAMA KINGS

DALMA HEYN

THE MEN WHO DRIVE

STRONG WOMEN

CRAZY...

DRAMA
KINGS

RODALE

Book design by Joanna Williams

Excerpt on pages 9–10 reprinted with permission of
Simon & Schuster Adult Publishing from *Moving Beyond Words* by Gloria Steinem.
Copyright © 1994 by Gloria Steinem.

Excerpt on page 190 from *The Seven Principles for Making Marriage Work*
by John M. Gottman, PhD, and Nan Silver.
Copyright © 1999 by John M. Gottman, PhD, and Nan Silver.
Used by permission of Crown Publishers, a division of Random House, Inc.

Library of Congress Cataloging-in-Publication Data

Heyn, Dalma.
    Drama kings : the men who drive strong women crazy / Dalma Heyn.
        p.   cm.
    Includes bibliographical references and index.
    ISBN-13 978–1–57954–888–9 hardcover
    ISBN-10 1–57954–888–1 hardcover
    1. Man-woman relationships. 2. Men—Attitudes. 3. Women—Life skills guides. I. Title.
HQ801.H474 2005
306.7—dc22   2005019535

Distributed to the trade by Holtzbrinck Publishers

2 4 6 8 10 9 7 5 3 1   hardcover

RODALE
LIVE YOUR WHOLE LIFE™

We inspire and enable people to improve their lives and the world around them

For more of our products visit **rodalestore.com** or call 800-848-4735

TO DIANA

*To care passionately for another human creature
brings always more sorrow than joy, but all the same,
Elinor, one would not be without that experience.*

—*Agatha Christie*, Sad Cypress

Contents

Preface xi

Acknowledgments xviii

Chapter One:
All the Kings' Women 1

Chapter Two:
Pleasing Women 19

Chapter Three:
Drama King #1: The Visitor 33

Chapter Four:
Drama King #2: The Proprietor 63

Chapter Five:
Drama King #3: The Easygoing Guy (EGG) 97

Chapter Six:
Drama King #4: The Hit-and-Run Lover 119

Chapter Seven:
Drama King #5: The Feeling-Impaired Guy (FIG) 153

Chapter Eight:
"Why Do They Stay?" 171

Chapter Nine:
When the Curtain Falls 183

Selected Bibliography 199

Index 202

Preface

We all know a Drama King. We've all dated one (or two or three). We've all had fun with one for a time. He can be so darling; so irresistible. Yet without necessarily being tyrannical, hysterical, or in any other way over the top (that's a drama *queen*), he creates intense melodrama in relationships and finally sabotages intimacy. A Drama King may cast a strong woman in the part of his leading lady, but he doesn't really want to share the spotlight, or even the stage. His anxiety over attachment, his discomfort with commitment, and his refusal to let go of outdated sex roles reveal his fatal flaw: *He cannot give a strong woman what she wants.*

A strong woman open to love is drawn to a Drama King for the same reasons she's drawn to other men: He may be handsome, successful, smart, seductive, and fun. His quirky intelligence may enchant her, his droll humor and laid-back manner move her, his sexual intensity thrill her, and his unconventional approach to life challenge her. Whatever his style, persistent or soft-sell, he's promising—so why would she turn him down? He doesn't *appear* troubled; he doesn't *look* damaged; he doesn't *declare* himself unfit for requited love; he doesn't *show* that he's nothing but trouble. No physical or emotional trait gives him away before the curtain opens, conveniently revealing his character before the relationship's first act. No program notes announce that his is always a one-man show. The strong woman doesn't cynically think to herself, "If he were fit for a relationship, he'd already be in one," or "Drama Kings are overrepresented in the pool of available men, so I'll pass on this cute guy." She expects neither to lose nor to be in the arms of a loser. So she takes him on.

Only as the plot unfolds does she see that what made him so attractive is also what makes him so toxic—that his boyish charm is really arrested development, his archetypal robustness an impenetrable wall, his masculine intensity a ticking time bomb, and his refreshing laid-backness a lack of feeling and an inability to connect. Only in the middle of the performance does her sweet hope of a juicy, lasting love story with the star evaporate—and turn into an ominous foreshadowing of a disastrous last act.

A Drama King grew up believing that the only thing required of him in an intimate relationship is to show up. A holdover from a time when the mere label "eligible bachelor" was sufficient to win hearts, he still assumes that his willingness to pick up a check is a potent aphrodisiac, that announcing that he's not gay is ample foreplay, and that simply being a single male makes him a great catch. Stuck in a my-needs-come-first understanding of relationships, he's surprised that it isn't all about *him* anymore. He doesn't care to hear why it's better for everyone, him included, that he's no longer the center of the universe; he still thinks he should be. So he will sulk, have a fit, withdraw, invade, evade, detach, bolt, or otherwise drive strong women crazy. But these strong women aren't putting up with it anymore.

In the past two decades, I've talked to hundreds of women— mostly middle class, self-sufficient, influential in their fields, of all faiths and colors—about their intimate relationships. Twenty and even ten years ago, the women I interviewed for my essays, articles, columns, and books spoke about a mysterious muting they experienced in love, a surprising, confusing loss of self that began inexorably soon after they entered close involvements, even as they stayed in love. When I wrote *The Erotic Silence of the American Wife* in 1992, I was stunned by the radical story I began to hear about the elusiveness of women's happiness inside the very institution—marriage—they thought was designed for it. There were no words then for such transgressive emotions. It didn't "make sense" for privileged middle-class women with work and husbands, homes and children, to be feeling such distress. Yet women all over the country spoke of a loss of pleasure so overwhelming it was akin to a loss of *themselves*—a fact missing from the literature about women and sex and love, and a phenomenon that altered my understanding of all three.

Five years later, in 1997, I heard the same story from even younger women. In *Marriage Shock: The Transformation of Women into Wives*, I tried to pinpoint the moment of this loss of pleasure. When and how does it break down? How does desire get shut off and delight extinguished? Tracing the incremental changes in newly-wed women, I found that the breakdown process didn't take long: It began right at the altar and developed fairly quickly into the unique malaise I call marriage shock. I believe that marriage shock, if unchecked, accounts for the unusually high rate of depression among young married women. Moreover, it begins to explain how it's possible that the most depressed group in our culture—wives—are living under the same roofs with the *least* depressed group—husbands!

I'm still interested in why intimate relationships so often en-liven men but exhaust women—but how things have changed! The hundred women I spoke with for this book have told me a star-tlingly different story—one with a happy (not happily-ever-after) ending. These women have careers, resources, self-esteem, deep friendships, and a bold new sense of entitlement and independence. They now have little tolerance for the incapacitating malaise I used to hear about and little inclination to let love, or anything else, mute their voices or endanger their selves. They're focused on their rich lives. They know how to work hard at relationships, but they know how to let go, too.

They tell a buoyant, if complicated, story of love in a time of chaos. In a climate rife with dire news about love and marriage; headlines blaring out stories of lurid affairs and hair-raising divorces; statistics threatening career-focused women with a lifetime of loneliness; and a zeitgeist featuring despairing women frantically hunting down sex, love, and marriage "before it's too late," these women are neither despairing nor frantic. In contrast to the stories popular culture is currently feeding them—tales of smart, high-achieving women living with and marrying men who grow fatter and more clueless with each new TV sitcom—they have ultimately rejected any script that features disappointment as their fate.

They have grown stronger.

Drama Kings have not.

Strong women have experienced living from their own centers; they know "the taste of the ocean," as the Buddha used to say. They have shed Old Relationships like outgrown skins and are "growing" in their place a desire for—an insistence on—something newer, suppler, and more encompassing for both partners than anything that has gone before.

Drama Kings are not.

In a world where "courtship" and "forever" are still habitually yearned for but are as outmoded and defunct as my old IBM XT, strong women have altered their fantasies of happily ever after. At a time when dating is no longer a lovely ritual preparatory to marriage but rather uncharted territory, a lawless landscape where hearts are broken nightly, and no tales of sense and sensibility offer guidance and explanation, strong women are adapting with humor and hope.

Drama Kings are not. And that is going to start costing them mightily.

These strong women I speak of are part of a large and growing phenomenon, the next leap in women's evolution. Long considered the "natural" relationship pros, they're now also gaining strength out in the world, where upper- and middle-class men once possessed all the power. As women painstakingly accrue the material strength they have lacked, Drama Kings have not kept up their end by developing the intimacy skills that *they* have lacked. It's as if these particular men are frozen in another, older drama of their own and are still reminiscing about the time when women filled their theaters nightly and applauded each performance, good or bad. Women, busy now with their own shows (not to mention those of their children and parents), can attend only a few of their actor-lovers' performances and no longer feel the need to applaud the flops. But the men you'll see in this book keep acting anyway, chewing up the scenery even as they watch their desperately needed audience leave the theater.

As any strong woman who's been dragged down and backward by a Drama King will tell you, a relationship can't move forward when it's anchored in the past. And the past is where he hangs out, meticulously avoiding the joy of writing something new and hopeful, a fabulous, adventurous love story. While loving a Drama King may temporarily call up everything in a woman that's both culturally and individually regressive—sapping the very strength she's so proud of—her stamina returns with surprising force once she's out of one of these depleting relationships. It's as if grappling with a Drama King were part of an emotional circuit-training program that's exhausting but worth it because the woman grows healthier, happier, and more resilient afterward. By recognizing him, experiencing him, and ultimately freeing herself from him, she's slowly working out a new way to be in relationships.

Strong women are thus bringing about cataclysmic social change. Their insistence that men develop more strength in relationships comes at the same time that Drama Kings feel their power slipping, both in the world and in love. While so many other men are putting their time and hearts into their intimate relationships, these men are not. Instead, as if their power and strength were being threatened, even usurped, they keep their distance.

In response to women's desire for a new paradigm of love that suits them better, a relationship into which they can bring their whole selves, the Drama King has become less, not more, flexible. Less, not more, available. Less, not more, adaptable. He's relationally shut down; he has crossed his arms over his chest and doesn't want to hear about it. He's chosen stonewalling over connection, isolation over intimacy, detachment over engagement. His response to a never-before-asked-of-him reciprocity and sharing of power—meaning money, decisions, housework, childcare, pleasure, and leisure—is a predictable "No."

Strong women want to hear "Yes"—so they move on.

You'd think a Drama King trying to make a comeback would change his ways before he meets his next lover and become an *ex*-Drama King. But in his fearful fantasies, strong women tend to be like those in *Kill Bill*; his secret yearning is for the decorous, demure, man-centric model of womanhood—as in *The Donna Reed Show*—that so many women have rejected. Where another man feeling left behind might look within himself for an explanation for the breakup, a Drama King is likely to move on to the next woman unchanged, unmoved, and unmindful. Feeling unmanned, he will then bring his buried rage into the next relationship—and the cycle will begin again.

Why can't he move forward? Why, if he loves her, won't he give a strong woman what she wants? And why does she stay—or does she?

More important, why is time spent with him not wasted, even though it ends (in anger, incredulity, sadness, laughter)? On the contrary, why is wrestling with a Drama King so much a part of a modern woman's experience, so apparently part of her emotional growth—and surviving a relationship with him one of the sources of her unparalleled new power?

These questions are at the heart of this book.

Women's very identity evidently feeds on time spent in a variety of relationships—stressful as well as blissful; fleeting as well as lasting. The core-deep, growing strength I see in the women I've spoken with appears to them and to me to be cumulative—building both through and because of their knotty and complicated involvements with all kinds of men, especially Drama Kings.

Acknowledgments

My greatest debt is to the women who spoke with me about their lives and their loves. Their involvement and openness were more than I could have hoped for. In addition to my interview subjects, I'd like to thank the many people with whom I had unrecorded conversations.

For offering their expertise, ideas, insights, and inspiration, I'm extremely grateful to Marion Asnes, Sunny Bates, Caprice Benedetti, Robert Berger, Alvin Blaustein, Gale Chaney, Andrew Cohen, Harriette Cole, the late Elizabeth Crow, Elizabeth Debold, Lesley Dormen, Peter Dunn, Trudy Festinger, Carol C. George, Jennifer George, Norval Glenn, Linda Gottlieb, Anne Heller, Ravenna Helson, Susan Kamil, Alison Knapp, Lynne Layton, Chazz Levi, Vikki Lucas, Brian McLendon, Andy McNichol, Barbara Perry Marek, Judy Miles, Valerie Monroe, Edris Nicholls, Amy O'Connor, Patricia O'Toole, Jonna Paolella, Bob Perkins, Ethel Person, Natalie Robins, Jessica Roemischer, Erika Schwartz, Deborah Siegel, Michelle Slung, Michael Steinberg, Judith Stone, Judith Thurman, and Beth Wareham.

My thanks, too, to the women at EnlightenNext, who opened their lives to me and shared their committed vision of bringing about evolutionary change and the role of relationships in it. I gained valuable information and inspiration from the speakers at the Omega Institute's Women and Power conferences and from the women there who generously shared their stories with me. I also benefited from attending the Smart Marriage conference in 2004 and from the discussions that came out of it.

My thanks to my researcher, Sally Clark, for her excellence, and to Diana Erney for her enthusiastic research assistance.

I'm thankful to Herb Marcucilli for his generous, much-needed zero-hour computer help.

For their valued comments on different drafts and their special contribution to this book, I'm indebted to Amy Cooper, Stephanie von Hirschberg, Olga Valdes, and Eileen Winnick.

My thanks to Amy Rhodes and Mariska van Aalst for embracing the project from beginning to end. Mariska, my editor, remained the book's protective midwife, even when moments away from giving birth to her daughter. Associate editor Amy Super took the manuscript over without missing a beat, and I'm very grateful to her.

For hours of conversation and thought that went to the heart of the book, I thank Kitty Ross.

My gratitude to my agent, Joni Evans, whose counsel and care are a daily blessing.

Very special thanks—yet again—to Annie Gottlieb for her immeasurable, indispensable contribution.

And my love and thanks to Richard, my husband, for freeing me from the specter of Drama Kings forever.

Chapter One

All the Kings' Women

Love me in full being.

—Elizabeth Barrett Browning, Love Poems

Maureen Fisher says she has it all.

At thirty-eight, she is healthy, the mother of an adored teenage son, Timothy, and the marketing director of the biggest sports equipment store in Florida. She and Timothy live in a small house forty minutes from Tampa. Timothy's father, Maureen's ex-husband, Christopher, lives close by, popping over several times a week when Maureen works late so Timothy won't be alone. Maureen's relationship with Christopher is good, now that their divorce is well behind them and Timothy's well-being is their only concern. She has three dear, close friends; a Tibetan terrier; and aging parents she is happy to support.

Has it all? Let's see: Did she forget to mention a man?

No, she didn't forget. Maureen knows she doesn't fit the picture of the woman she was supposed to have become at her age, complete with the lifetime husband, or lifetime partner, or a potential one, or at least *someone*. Yet there is no one on the horizon, and she is as content as can be. She's not even looking.

I only began to recognize that I'm truly happy—maybe even happiest—without a guy when I did some serious thinking about what's right for me. I had to deconstruct all the myths about women's happiness; challenge all the assumptions, the promises, the dreams laid out for me by my family, my friends, even the stories I grew up on. I had to learn to read those newspaper items— "Distraught Woman Can't Find Man!" "Unmarried Woman Shoots Self!" Because not to have a man at thirty-eight means I don't have the one thing I've been told all my life is the only *thing. So for that part of me that was taught I'm not a full human being without this "other half," it's like having a missing psychic limb.*

But that's programming, not my own reaction, and I'm not manipulated anymore. I've been with a slew of goofy guys, and I didn't want to stay with any of them. Some were appealing, some tyrannical, and some just ridiculous; some were fun and sexy and wild; and some were not so good for Timothy. I went through sadness, weirdness, desperation, until it hit me like a slap: I don't have to try so hard to be in a relationship! I don't have to suffer for a man! *I live wonderfully without any of them!*

I'm not saying forever on this—I love men, I love sex. I love being in love. But I've found the notion *of one* man *way more appealing than the reality of being with any of the men I've been out with.*

Tracy, at thirty, feels enormous pressure to marry a man she's dated for almost a year but who she nevertheless believes is "clueless" about her. She's a loan officer for a commercial bank in Topeka; he's a musician a few years younger. All her friends are either already married or about to be. She says it takes everything she's got to ward off the onslaught of advice about how best to transform Dan—the "pretty crazy" guy she "sort of" loves—into husband material.

> *I hear about having relationship talks, playing hard to get, giving him ultimatums, dumping him outright—the thing is, it's all like Republicans talking to Democrats: See, I don't want what they want. I don't want to bludgeon him into understanding me any more than I want him bludgeoning me into understanding him.*
>
> *I'm in the most conservative business in the world in a very conservative town. I wear little navy suits to work and pumps with clear panty hose. Dan looks like Nick Nolte in one of his drunk-driving mug shots, with the hair, the wild eyes, the dissolute bit. But here's the thing. He calls and says, "Hey! Let's go hiking today," or wakes me up at 6 a.m. on a Saturday after a gig with, "I fixed our bikes. Let's go for a ride." I love that. We don't talk much, except about practical stuff—the amount of air in the tires, the best conditions for hiking. He expresses his emotions through his guitar and physical activity.*

And *her* emotions?

Tracy enjoys wrestling with her own complicated, contradictory feelings "all by myself"—another thing that confounds her friends.

I don't need to share my ambivalence or investigate his. I don't need to beat ambiguity and doubt into submission—I can live with it. I don't require Dan to understand my messy psyche. Who says a man is supposed to understand me? Who says a man and woman can't get enough from each other by having fun together? And who says I have to marry or have children?

Well, she concedes quickly with a grin, pretty much everyone. But that's their problem, she believes. "I love kids, but I may not want one of my own."

So when friends ask her when she's going to get serious, she tells them she's very serious—just not about turning this good-enough-for-the-moment Drama King into Mr. Right. She's done three things that help, she says. "One, I broke out of the mold that says love is forever. Two, I broke out of the mold that says I'm supposed to be pushing marriage on any bachelor I find. And three, I broke out of the mold that says being alone is being lonely."

She wants, these days, to have fun. Her old craving for what she calls a love twin, a soul mate, feels regressive to her now, "like something I hunger for when I'm feeling the weakest and the most needy, a throwback to a time when there was no such thing for women as a life of one's own." Her desire for a soul mate is most intense, in other words, when it's an attempted shortcut to, or substitute for, a soul of her own.

She lives in the moment and has learned to love doing things by herself. She knows she's with a Drama King and accepts it for now.

There are things I can't stand about our relationship, and others that I may never get again: He's sort of a lunatic—not sort-of; really a lunatic—and I put up with a lot of unprocessed stuff from him, a lot of narcissism and aggression. But then, sex

is great; he's a passionate guy. And unlike every other man I've
met, he likes me exactly the way I am—and I'm a moody, cranky,
bossy thing. He doesn't call me selfish for putting myself first in
my life, and he doesn't attack me for sounding—as I often do, I'm
told—like it's my way or the highway.

Tracy sums up what feels new to her about herself. "I'm the real
me. I don't do what I'm told; I do what feel. And my life has taken
off. I don't *need* a man. And not needing Dan has freed me to . . .
want him."

Anabel has been married and divorced and remarried and divorced—from the same man. Now, at forty-four, she has gone
out with "every conceivable kind of maniac" and continues to do so
with gusto, convinced that "that's what's out there." She loved being
married, "or else I wouldn't have tried so hard with Frank," her on-
again-off-again ex-husband. As for wedlock again, though, she's in
no hurry "to get back on *that* horse. When people say, 'What a pity
you're not married; you'd make someone a great wife,' I tell them
that my greatness as a wife isn't the point. That 'someone's' greatness as a husband *is.*" She sees no man in her troupe of Drama
Kings that qualify. Still, she's always up for a relationship that is—
she rolls her eyes heavenward—"healthy" and "normal."
And this, she says, is the problem.

The healthier I get, the more self-sufficient and contented I
am that way, the more I seem to attract the world's wackos. There
was Tom, the most commitment-phobic yet most desperately

needy-but-God-forbid-he-admit-it kind of guy, who kept saying how uncomplicated he was but kept falling asleep at dinner and going home by 8:30. There was Harry, the chef, who made me feel I was too inept to go near my own cutting board with a knife in my hand. There was Jon, who came over at noon every day for a month, whether invited or not. Wouldn't stay. Just deposited his white van, which looked disturbingly like O.J. Simpson's, in my driveway at lunchtime for a nooner. Come to think of it, he even looked like a young O.J."

Anabel, who says she identifies with a slew of pop-culture heroines—from Carrie in *Sex and the City* to Donna Moss in *The West Wing* to Grace in *Will and Grace*—is a dermatologist in Houston. She's considering coming out with her own makeup line, and Estée Lauder is interested already. She has three black Labs and two Siamese cats. Attractive men, she says, are always welcome into her menagerie—for lunch or whatever—but will never replace it.

What I can't get over is that the more stable and confident I become, the more content with my own life, the more I'm open to something new and healthy and positive and equal in a relation-ship—the lack of neediness men have long claimed they want, after all—the more the men seem to regress and try to drag me back to some old dynamic I thought we were all through with. Then, when these bizarre relationships end, I keep going forward, growing stronger and stronger—but the men keep going back-ward in time! So there I am, suddenly, feeling like on the one hand I'm Xena, Warrior Princess, but once in a relationship, I'm like Anna with the King of Siam, expected to bow lower than he does.

What convinces her that she's gaining strength and going forward after these "bizarre" relationships end?

Well, I'm successful, for one thing. And I feel better after each guy. I have more fun, incrementally. I constantly shed old stuff and feel cleaner, leaner, clearer. Even if I feel punched in the stomach for a few days and take to my bed over a weekend or two, I'm not devastated, not at my core. I feel like those cartoon characters who fall head first into the pavement, get smashed flat, then jump right up, shake themselves off, and go zooming into the next adventure.

Look: I just bought a house! I love it and I'm proud of myself and I love my weird life and I don't care that I'm house poor and without a guy. I don't see myself as failing, you see, but as succeeding. I don't see the end of a relationship as some moral deficiency on my part. I'm getting the hang of love's . . . temporariness. I've grown big time in terms of how I relate to men. In college, in the dorms, I mothered the guys and picked up their stupid socks and tried to help them grow up. Now I don't. If I decide to see a guy, I take him as he is. And if he lives like a slob or behaves like a child, I don't go there. And if he's altogether horrible, I let him go.

What you're hearing here is a cosmic change in women's attitudes toward relationships. If I had heard one woman speak the way Maureen, Tracy, and Anabel do when I was researching my last book, I would have thought I was in another country. Back then, in the mid-1990s, I heard women tell stories of the unassailable centrality of their intimate relationships, an importance that dwarfed everything else in their lives. I did not hear anyone say she believed that moving through a succession of temporary, imperfect relationships might be a good thing. Women spoke of turning themselves inside out to make even the least satisfying pairings function, obsessing over loves that often limped painfully toward the elusive "forever" they swore to attain—because to not reach it would have left them with a sense of failure, despair, and loneliness. They sometimes spent their entire adult lives in unions in which they felt afraid to speak honestly, dissembling for years, for lifetimes, because their deepest feelings did not fit what they were told they "should" be.

In the mid '90s, I listened to women who struggled to bring their true selves with them into intimate relationships; who were unable to negotiate the desperate impasses they experienced with their men but nevertheless clung to relationships to avoid the loneliness and stigma of being alone. The last thing I could then imagine was women feeling sanguine about impermanence; upbeat about being plunged into a bewildering and chaotic mating climate; buoyant when giving up on a guy or even being "dumped" by him; increasingly finding strength and joy within themselves and in their friendships, their homes, and their careers—and not dependent on an intimate relationship for those qualities.

Suddenly, I'm hearing women speak of growing stronger through relationships, even the ones that end; of finding themselves afterward feeling okay, hopeful, and even ebullient—and game for more. I'm not hearing about "failed" relationships or long-lasting devastation when relationships are over but about successful adventures, meaningful—if oddball—experiences; relationships that, even as they lurch, founder, and sink, leave the woman feeling freer, savvier, and more self-aware.

This is not to say a woman doesn't crave relationships or remain pain-free when they end—only that she increasingly doesn't wholly depend on them, as her mother or even her older sister might have, for her self-esteem, identity, or solvency. Even as the culture continues instilling a fear in her that each man may be her last, urging that she push to land him any way she can, she sees her divorced mother dating, her workaholic father dating, her widowed *grandparents* dating—so she doesn't believe it. She is one of the eighty-six million single adults who may soon define the country's new majority, so she has company in imagining life, even if temporarily, on her own. She is willing to hold out longer for the kind of relationship she wants—that, or go it alone.

Whereas I once heard denial about divorce—young women whose parents had divorced nevertheless insisting it could never happen to them—I now hear a more clearheaded understanding of the new meaning of forever. And where I once heard fantasies of being rescued financially and emotionally, I now hear anything but. In fact, I hear the opposite: a growing fear of having to emotionally *and* financially rescue men. Where I once heard open despair about the disappearance of courtship—with its comforting, well-worn cultural rituals and milestones that led clearly to marriage—I now hear about resilience and courage in the face of its loss. As Gloria Steinem, whose voice has so often presaged that of the next generation, puts it:

> *I used to indulge in magical thinking when problems seemed insurmountable. Often, this focused on men, for they seemed to me the only ones with power to intercede with the gods. Now it*

has been so long since I fantasized a magical rescue that I can barely remember the intensity of that longing. Instead, I feel my own strength, take pleasure in the company of mortals, and no longer believe in gods. Except those in each of us.

The loss of what love used to be, or might have been, is more than compensated by women's sense of having done vital internal work to build themselves, their *selves*—work that will serve them in their *next* relationships. They don't, in other words, feel stuck in this place of pain or loss; they move past it quickly. Something deep in the culture and deep in women has shifted—and it's an extraordinary, evolutionary shift. The man-centric view of the world has been realigned by today's women, and the effect of men's displacement from it is as revolutionary as when Copernicus squashed the notion that the Earth was flat.

It happened so quickly. The stories I used to hear from women in the 1980s, 1990s, and even a few years ago were so often about understanding, reforming, revamping, or redeeming men. I don't mean simply that love was important to them. Women valued relationships over themselves—as if, I sometimes thought, having a relationship with a man, any relationship, was felt to be crucial to an intact self, prerequisite to it. Hanging on to a Drama King, no matter how unhappy he made her, no matter how paltry his emotional and financial offering, was more important than being happy.

As Wendy, married at twenty-two and startled by her husband's increasing disengagement, put it a year ago, "His stonewalling makes *me* feel unvalued. It makes *me* feel unloved. So I try to make him talk instead of hiding out, but he only shuts up more—a response that only makes me feel worse."

Until recently, their stories featured an old, familiar dilemma: While men felt the pressure to be strong providers or else be accused of being failures, women felt the pressure to be selfless nurturers—relationship "experts" responsible for the well-being of a couple and fixing whatever ailed it—or else be accused of being failures at the one job they were supposed to do "naturally." Men felt uncomfortably bound to the workplace and women to their relationships—regardless of how much they might have wished that they could *share* both. If this setup left women powerless in the world, it left men relationally inept, devoid of the skills to connect with the women they loved. If women couldn't single-handedly break through to their isolated, conquering heroes, the men became angry, bereft, guilty, and more isolated. As Connie, a woman who appeared in both of my previous books, recently recalled:

> *I could not make him, the man who supposedly loved me, understand me. He could not hear me. Hey, he couldn't even listen to me. Or wouldn't; I never could tell. He was a lawyer, and I swear, unless I spoke in lawyerese—cited numbers to prove my argument, revealed statistics to back up an idea—he didn't believe me! I became mute as a wastebasket.*

Not so today. Connie has since left her lawyer, one of the more tyrannical types of Drama Kings. Now, she talks her head off to a man who wants to understand, a man who is listening, hearing, responding, and trying his best to develop the skills to be as fully inside the relationship as she is. She couldn't have it any other way.

Or take Wendy, who said about her new marriage in my first book:

> *When do I start being myself? When does this relationship start to be as intimate and easy and happy as it promised to be? When does Ben start talking to me a lot, the way all the men I've known always did? It took a year for me to get it through my head that this was it.*

This was it, and it was her life; it was everything.

Wendy left her marriage at age forty, surprising everyone—including Ben, her shut-down, emotion-avoidant Drama King. She is now happily single, running the trust and estates division of the bank at which she's worked for twenty years. She is closer, now, to her two grown children. She says, as if to reassure me, that it's possible she would consider sharing her home with someone again but that she's in no hurry because she's happier than she's ever been.

I'd spent years hearing stories about the transformation of women into wives, and now I was hearing about the transformation of wives into women. And their stepping stones? Drama Kings.

I watch this sea change in awe. We've gone from the time when women placed relationships, no matter how bad, first above all else, to a time when they express surprise and joy at odd-shaped, unscripted lives in which they feel complete even without an overweening love interest. That women today are on another beat, led by a drummer from a wild new rhythm section that's quite different from the one that used to move them, is borne out by research. Girls have powered ahead startlingly. Girls are surpassing boys at every level in undergraduate and graduate schools. Women, who became the majority of American college students more than twenty years ago, now make up fifty-seven percent of college students. According to *Newsweek*, they also get more out of college: They're more likely to study abroad, join in activities like community service, and seek counseling for problems. They are less likely to transfer, drop out, or even commit suicide than their male college classmates. As recently as the 1970s, men tended to "marry down" educationally; today, with women who receive bachelor's and master's degrees surpassing the number of men who do—a trend presumed to continue, according to the National Center for Education Statistics—wives may soon routinely be more highly educated than their mates. This trend, according to Elaina Rose, PhD, associate professor of economics at the University of Washington in Seattle, also reverses what's called hypergamy, in which the most highly educated women were left most often without husbands. Today, according to Dr. Rose, "the rate at which men marry up is about equal to the rate at which women marry up."

There are now twice as many women ages twenty to thirty-four in the work force as there were in 1970, and their financial assets are expected to rise dramatically in the coming years. Surveys vary as to how many men now have women partners who are the sole breadwinners, but some say as many as one in five. Although women still make seventy-six cents to men's dollar, a huge percentage of wealth is in women's hands: Forty-three percent of Americans with more than $500,000 in assets are women. The annual income in households headed by women grew twenty-nine percent from 1993 to 2000—the biggest jump among all households. The Securities Industry Association estimates that 220,000 women head households with incomes of more than $100,000, a number expected to double by 2010, when they'll control more than $1 trillion in assets.

Not only are female high achievers everywhere, but single men expect it. The strong woman is everywhere researchers look. "Today's woman can run, swim, and skate faster than any man of a few decades ago, and the gap that does exist may soon close," writes Barbara Ehrenreich, who goes on to point out in *Newsweek* that women also seem to be more resistant to fatigue and can outlast men in physical endurance races. In the sheer longevity race, women win by seven years. Women surpass all previous assumptions about their mental as well as physical capacities and now live up to dictionary definitions of the word *strong*—both the *Merriam-Webster Dictionary*'s "those who wield force, authority, or influence" and the *Concise Oxford English Dictionary*'s "those who are able to withstand great force or opposition; not easily damaged or overcome."

In all areas—physical, emotional, educational, athletic, psychological, and spiritual—women triumph, because women today have more power than ever before over their own lives and therefore over their relationships. As renowned psychoanalyst Ethel Person, MD, speaks of it, "To possess personal power is to be truly in possession of the self, to be able to use oneself as the instrument of one's own plans." To which I would add, the instrument of one's own pleasure as well. "When we possess [personal power]," she goes on to say, "we feel sure of ourselves; when we exercise it, we feel a kind of high."

These women do feel a kind of high, for what this has meant in their relationships is a shift that would be unrecognizable to their grandparents. Women have gone from a primary need to please men—for fear that if they didn't, they'd be left alone and destitute—to a desire to explore on their own, have fun, experience life. Seeing love through their own eyes rather than seeing themselves through others' more critical eyes, they can now search not just for a suitable match but for someone who will please *them*.

One of the themes in my earlier books is the confusion modern middle-class women felt not only between selflessness and selfishness but also between pleasing and pleasure, for ours was a culture that urged them not only to please or else lose but also to believe that pleasing others *was* women's pleasure. In my interviews in the 1980s and 1990s, women actually conflated the two words and, more to the point, judged themselves harshly for finally teasing them apart and for choosing wanting for themselves *over* giving to others. "What more could you possibly want?" the question went, the one in their heads, the one society asked, "when you already have everything a woman should want?" This internalized conundrum kept them from knowing, let alone voicing and pursuing, their true desires. When they considered getting their happiness in ways more direct than by giving, they had visions not of happy independence but of loss of love.

Women don't isolate pleasure from power, as if they were different worlds, but tend to unite the two. They see power as something that includes pleasure—in fact, for the women I've spoken with, pleasure *is* power. Delighting in work, love, home, colleagues, children, lovers, and themselves, with time for all—that's power. Rather than thinking of power as something one person gains at the expense of another, or a relationship in which one has it and one doesn't, women think of it as something shared.

But two people can't share power if one doesn't want to.

I've heard some wildly romantic, sexy, soulful stories about Drama Kings: After all, these are often attractive men who really do sweep women off their feet. Antiheroes they may be, but who says they aren't sometimes more initially thrilling than heroes? How exciting they are!—for a time. Some of them are the stuff of our entire notion of love. Think of literature without Heathcliff—"Rough as a saw-edge and hard as whinstone. The less you meddle with him, the better." (No, Cathy wouldn't meddle for long, but she did lament, "Whatever our souls are made of, his and mine are the same.") Think of poetry without Lord Byron, whom Lady Caroline Lamb declared "mad, bad and dangerous to know" or film without Rhett Butler—King of Drama Kings—who, when he met Scarlett, "grinned maliciously as a tomcat, and again his eyes went over her, in a gaze totally devoid of the deference she was accustomed to."

Part of our attraction to Drama Kings is that they live in our collective unconscious (think Othello, Don Giovanni, King Lear, for starters—or even modern entries, like Big in *Sex and the City*)—for aren't stormy, jealous, unreliable, brooding, good-timin', evasive, or impenetrable men the ones we grew up believing were "romantic"? Weren't they what surrounded us? Well, Drama Kings can be all that and more. Their instinct, after all, is the same as all men's: to love women; to want love, pleasure, and happiness. They just can't pull it off. And they know it. So they *act* as if they can, for as long as they can.

Drama Kings, alas, cannot share power, because they are too afraid of losing it. In their schema, if one person has it, another does not—and they don't want to be the latter. They cannot share the parts of themselves that intimacy requires. Their inner lives, their particular wounds, family dynamics, and psychologies, might give us some insight into why they feel compelled to act as they do. But frankly, as interesting as their psyches are to examine, they needn't concern us here. I believe that we've all spent too long analyzing and justifying Drama Kings' behavior. We've blamed their mothers, their fathers, their hormones; blamed their fragile masculinity, television, the school system, and everything else. We've examined their brains, their libidos, their vulnerabilities, their fears, their fantasies, their unexpressed childhood traumas. We've noticed that when they're depressed, they don't seek help. We've noticed that they become murderous and suicidal when their lovers leave them. We've kept hidden our knowledge of their unexpressed dependency on us. We've pretended not to see their fragility and their shame. We've protected them. We've become Women Who

Understand Too Much—and I don't want to be one of them, nor do I encourage you to be.

For it's not Drama Kings' experience of the world I'm interested in here; it's strong women's experience of them. It's not Drama Kings' psyches I want to explore but how women's psyches develop while loving them. It's not whether Drama Kings will ever learn; it's what women are learning from them.

The women in this book speak less about one man forever than of a succession of men over time—men who may not last long but whose lessons in love are lasting. About half of the women I spoke with began dating before they were sixteen and, in keeping with the national average, had their first experience of sexual intercourse when they were seventeen. Some married at twenty-eight—again, the national average—and some didn't. Either way, they had at least a decade of sexual and relational experimentation. Journalist and social historian Barbara Dafoe Whitehead, PhD, has observed that early adult love relationships have come to resemble early career development, a "high-turnover but low-commitment pattern" of "instructive, memorable, but short-term arrangements."

The women I interviewed spoke cheerfully, gamely, and humorously, if ruefully, not of a Mr. Right but of a festival of Mr. Wrongs—of Drama Kings—much as they would catalog the learning opportunities in a succession of jobs they were thrilled to have had, but only for a while. Freud's infamous question, "Women, what do they want?" which he believed was shrouded in darkness, is being answered without hesitation by women who easily enumerate it: to be themselves; to be complete; to have interesting, productive lives; to be in thriving relationships that suit them as well as their men and their children; to be *the agents of their own pleasure*. Increasingly, they want all of the above.

A woman may now choose to live alone or with a man, a woman, or a family—in or out of wedlock. She may have a child or not, in wedlock or not, through the usual method of conception or not. She may raise a child alone or in a biological family or in a "family" she chooses: with one man or one woman or a friend or a parent or with a group of friends. She may, if she's not ready for or undecided about having a child, freeze her eggs and push her biological clock forward into her forties or even later. (According to the Rutgers Marriage Project's "State of Our Unions," young girls have become less traditional in their views about legitimate lifestyles, increasingly accepting either living on their own or cohabiting. Even more than boys, today's teenage girls accept single motherhood as a way to live, calling out-of-wedlock childbearing a worthwhile lifestyle.)

She may well live with or marry a man younger than she—particularly, according to the Current Population Survey, if it's her second marriage. Or she may not marry, and she may not live with anyone. If she does wish to marry, she can designate a pal clergy for a day to conduct the ceremony. There's no consensus on how she should conduct herself. Whatever choice she makes, regardless of whether some people disapprove or whether it's the option she would choose in the best of all possible worlds, she will rarely lose her job or her friends or her honor because of her choice. She will not be, as she once would surely have been, hurled to the margins of society. All that is over.

The change took hundreds of years—and less than a decade.

Chapter Two

Pleasing Women

A woman will always sacrifice herself if you give her the opportunity. It's her favorite form of self-indulgence.

—W. Somerset Maugham, The Circle

The year is 1790, and Thomas Jefferson writes to his newly married daughter, Martha Randolph: "The happiness of your life depends now on continuing to please a single person; to this all other objects must be secondary." That person is, of course, her new husband. Thirteen years after that, in 1803, another bride's father, a pastor named Dean Swift, appoints himself his daughter's "director" in a project of making herself "worthy" of her new husband, promising to let her know "how you are to act, and what you are to avoid." Devoted fathers all over America were penning similar letters to their marriageable or just-married daughters, solemnly instructing them on their conduct in love and wedlock. They said, in one way or another, "Pleasing is serious business, my darling girl. You will have no home, no money, no social standing, no *life*—unless you become as irrevocably ensconced in the home of another man as you have been in mine, and ensure that you're just as cherished."

The theme of winning and keeping a man soon became the focus of a genre of letters, pamphlets, and books aptly called conduct books, primers for pleasing that took over from these anxious dads' letters. These books became astonishingly popular in America and England at the dawn of the middle class, each one pouring out, as if from a deranged spigot, urgent advice to women.

Overnight, love—an activity that you'd think takes at least two—was defined solely as a woman's job. Men and women, accustomed until then to sharing their social, political, work, and home lives, with each participating in all four, were for the first time isolated from each other—men hurled into the industrial workplace and women banished into the home, alone. The indispensable work women once did—planting and preserving food, creating cloth and clothes, handling all manner of economic production—was now relegated to factories, and the age-old dynamic between useful men and women was instantly changed forever. Conduct books, despite their lofty, euphemistic titles—"The Lady's New Year's Gift," "A Father's Legacy to His Daughters," "The Young Lady's Friend"—began as exacting manuals on chimney cleaning and domestic hygiene. But they quickly morphed into less prosaic pamphlets with a goal of transforming women into the opposite of men—beacons of love; icons of selflessness, sympathy, compassion, virtue, accommodation, and chastity. Moreover, conduct books urged them to delight in and bring cheerfulness to the daunting new role and the newly divined "feminine" nature. The books' mission—to excise women from the business of the outside world, a world they once occupied as naturally as men, and to excise the concerns of the world from the women—was a sober one. Suddenly, there really was no other story for a woman's life.

In the changing, brutal world of capitalism's beginning, where a man could for the first time make rather than inherit money, a woman emphatically could not. She could be a factory slave or a prostitute or a governess, perhaps, but her only sure hope of sexual, physical, and financial safety was in one of these men's homes, as his wife. It thus fell to the self-appointed authors of conduct books to urge young women to embrace what they could earn: *love*. Jean Jacques Rousseau's dictum, "A woman's thoughts, beyond the range of her immediate duties, should be directed to the study of men," became a matter of her survival.

You begin to get the drift: As men's daily work became completely severed from cooperative relationships and turned into competitive ones, women's daily work became about cooperation to the exclusion of all else. As men's strength became all about worldly power—their power over other men—women assumed all the emotional strength, a strength centered on caring for, propping up, and overseeing the morals of faulty men, fragile children, the sickly, and the elderly. "You have deep responsibilities; you have urgent claims; a nation's moral worth is in your keeping," exclaimed author Sarah Ellis in 1839 in a book on women. No other delight was permitted to them. Any tinge of "selfishness" was considered so unloving, so unfeminine and unappreciative, it could cost them a man—and a life. Desperation as much as exhortation filled the air when, in 1847, an author calling herself Mrs. John Farrar (no credential other than the "Mrs." mattered) wrote, "Love in the heart of a wife should partake largely of the nature of *Gratitude*. She should fill her soul with Gratitude to God and to the Man who has chosen *her* to be his helpmate for time and for Eternity."

Conduct books laid out other ingredients then as plainly as a chef on the Food Network does now, and chopped them up as finely: Who she should be; how she should act; what she should do, feel, think, read, wear, say, and believe. Nothing was left to chance. What did a woman want? To become a wife, however absurd the recipe. As trumped-up and wheedling and hysterical as some of the proffered advice sounds to us now, nothing about the message was trivial. For a woman, it was not about having it all. It was all she had.

Three hundred years after Jefferson's letter to Martha, long after women got the vote, long after the introduction of the Pill, long after the women's movement and *Roe v. Wade*, you'd think there would have been seismic changes on the pleasing vs. pleasure front and that women would have greeted the notion of being seen as "selfish" with the same shrug most men do. But as recently as the late 1990s, when I wrote my last book, those changes were astonishingly few.

At an apartment near Barnard College in New York City in 1997, I listened to a group of young women in their twenties and thirties speak of love. Some were graduates I'd spoken with at the school in the early '90s, when they were still students. Now, older, their love stories varied: Many were merely hooking up occasionally; others were hanging out with men they'd at first hooked up with; some were dating; and a few were in committed, sexually exclusive intimate relationships. The men they were with were as varied as the stories, a cross-section of their gender who shared one trait only: Whether they articulated it openly or not, they expected their women to conform to them, not the other way around.

Delila was a 25-year-old honors graduate in women's studies with a master's degree in communications from the University of Michigan, a television whiz kid and a segment producer on a hot prime-time newsmagazine show. She began speaking about her year-long live-in relationship with a man named Michael: "I love him," she said, and then stopped short. "But I feel this weird tension between us about my really having my own life."

A hush of recognition fell over the group; the women pulled their chairs closer. Delila paused, started a few sentences, amended and then retracted them, and finally whispered, "When I'm at home with him, I sometimes feel I'm in the wrong place—like I'm not really me, like I don't belong there. It scares me, because while I'm not planning to leave or anything, I worry that the longer I stay, the more I'll dwindle away."

Looking at this splendid big-boned woman with clear green eyes and heavy, long blonde hair, feeling her wit and intelligence and energy, it was strange to hear her use the same vocabulary as the fictional Nora did in *A Doll's House*. The women called it "this *thing* that happens with men"—and had observed their friends, the ones in relationships, speak more softly or defer politely or even give up their views entirely when their lovers were in the room. Alternatively, these friends would speak more loudly, as if to counter the impulse to silence themselves. In order to focus on the relationship, the women in the room felt they surrendered what made them strong and authentic—their views and their feelings—and let slide many of the things they did for fun, the activities that made them feel good.

When I spoke to the group again in 1999, their fears had materialized. Delila, in some form representative of them all, had unwittingly, incrementally, become more careful, more self-censoring, more motherly—"sort of 'Should I be doing more for him?

Should I be monitoring his calorie intake? Be more in touch with his mother?' " she said. The specter of a specific kind of maternal selflessness, of pleasing, of "earning" love through goodness, hovered over them as it had over so many other women I'd spoken with. At this point, I'd begun to think that the ghost of womanhood past would always haunt us, no matter how hard we tried to banish it. "All I know is that doing things for him was always on my mind, as if it was my responsibility as a good girlfriend to make his life perfect," Delila admitted.

The other women nodded in sympathy. "Does this happen automatically?" they wondered. "Or do some men bring out something antiquated in us?"

Certainly every woman I spoke with during the writing of this book understood the conflict inherent in choosing pleasure over pleasing; many had experienced firsthand the sting of being thought "selfish" simply by dint of abdicating the role of pleaser. They often felt the impulse to be overly compliant and to try too hard to please, and they recognized the announcement of self-betrayal in their bellies when they did so.

It still happens, even today. Arriving like a bewildering betrayal, an unexpected blow to their innermost core, this hard-to-explain phenomenon that these women recognized and spoke of was all bound up in love, all knotted up inside relationships, no matter how different the details, no matter how varied the men. The women were experiencing a strange paradox: The hard-won self-realization and self-scrutiny that made them authentic, outspoken, truthful, and fit for intimacy seemed to become endangered once wedged inside relationships. It was as though goodness tried to possess them, as though Jefferson's letter to Martha, with all the fear for her that his warning contained, still coursed through their bloodstreams.

And the men, expecting no more and nothing less, were satisfied.

January 2005. I was embroiled in research for this book, surrounded by tapes, e-mails, and letters and occupied with scheduled interviews with a broad range of women of all ages, haunted by their experiences with Drama Kings. One busy morning, Delila called, wanting to come in to catch up. I decided to get the group together again, and she delightedly agreed. I had often wondered how they were, those gleaming young women so puzzled by the shift in their authenticity when they were around men.

It felt like old home week; laughter filled my office with Karen, a children's book editor in San Francisco; Eleanor, an African American cardiologist in Chicago; Delila; Kim, a Korean physical therapist in New York; Aisha, the promotion director for an athletic footwear firm, and Tandy, a fashion model from Norway. They had changed, lost that slightly blurry-around-the-edges look. Their clothes, once shrouds of loose black tops over baggy cargo pants and basketball sneakers, were still casual but more colorful and formfitting. "Note the absence of the all-black look," Kim said, as if reading my mind, and, throwing her acid-green bag onto the couch, she pointed with the fingers of both hands to her delicate kitten-heeled shoes.

The last time we spoke, Delila was struggling to hold on to her relationship but at the same time be herself in it. I asked her to start us off. She began to speak about Michael, the man she was now married to—briefly.

> I knew he wanted me to be independent, theoretically anyway, and I was convinced he was a man who truly liked me and was comfortable around women. He'd patiently waited such a long time for me.
>
> But once we lived together, this constant tension moved in. I was quickly cast as the eager-beaver closeness maven, and he was always backing off. I don't know how it happened, that dynamic.

It felt automatic, like we were both brainwashed and helpless to get deprogrammed. I'd try to tell him what I was feeling, and he'd look baffled or bemused or irritated. And there we were: pushy, needy broad; withholding, stonewalling guy. I'd say, "Look at what's happening! It's not really us! How do we fix this?" and he'd get annoyed, like, "Oh, who cares. Just . . . get off it."

I'd press: "Get off it? I'm trying to save us!"

He'd say, "Just leave it alone. We're fine."

As he'd shut down, my voice would rise, frantic with frustration that he could just leave it like that; that he thought we really were fine. He'd look pained and disapproving. And that would be that. Discussion over!

He once said outright, as if he were summing up everything he felt, "You're just too . . ." And he couldn't finish the sentence.

Just too. Too big, too much, too wanting, too whatever. At first, I thought he meant too successful, since I always worried that my career was going to be a sore point for us, but that wasn't the whole thing—in fact, he didn't bring that up, since I was helping to pay off his college debt! Then I thought he meant too controlling, but I rarely was; that isn't my nature. No, it was just me that was too! The more I was myself, the more I overwhelmed him, as though my very personality was too strong, or as though I was taking his strength or something. So at first I tried to make myself smaller, more palatable to him; hid all sorts of feelings; tried not to sound pushy or needy or wanting, or, shit, alive.

There it is once again, just as Delila framed it years before: women's ancient struggle to figure out how to have their full range of feelings and, at the same time, their connection with their men; to be loving and attentive, but not, as in the Somerset Maugham epigraph at the beginning of this chapter, self-sacrificing; to be communicative but not verbose; to be neither selfish nor selfless. Although the line between these opposite traits is clear to women in any other context, it seems to blur and become tricky to negotiate once they're in love. I have asked hundreds of women this simple question, "Can you be yourself in an intimate relationship?" and they have looked at me as if I were posing a Zen riddle. They have answered, "No, not with a man still reading from an ancient script. Not with a man threatened by a woman's strength and independence. Not with a man terrified of change." Not with a Drama King.

To Delila, connecting with Michael meant being authentic and honest and open—but to be that vulnerable made her appear too needy. Expressing her true desires made her appear too voracious—in short, too much. She sensed that her very existence felt to Michael on the one hand like a glorious gift but on the other like an impossible demand—one he could not, would not, fill. Unfortunately for her, being cast as the "demanding one" carried over into the bedroom. "Michael's sexuality didn't allow for a lusty wife," she said, echoing the experience of many married women I speak with. "Sadly, what his fantasy craved, his penis did not."

And here's where loving a Drama King becomes so difficult. Drama Kings want strong women's full attention but won't fully engage. They want strong women's love but feel easily overwhelmed. They want strong women's sexuality but shrink from it. They want strong women's earning power but resent the necessary focus on work that it entails. They take issue with their perceived diminishing clout at home and at work but don't want to talk about or deal with it. They feel women may be responsible for it, and they don't care that they act out their anger. Three-quarters of the women I spoke with said that the more they and their partners talked about what was going on between them, in or out of a therapist's office, the more their words zoomed by each other, like jets flying at different altitudes.

These women's stories shed light on why thirty years of marital counseling have brought this country a paltry one percent decrease in the divorce rate. Although I'm the trained psychotherapist, it was Delila who brought me this tragic statistic, announcing it when she told me she had given up and was divorcing Michael. Like other strong women, she finds Drama Kings overtly applauding her ambition, sensuality, achievement, and income but covertly still pressuring her to be the selfless, nurturing creature from the conduct books. Strong women find Drama Kings confused by women's more frankly expressed sexual desire, depending on but daunted by it and—perhaps as a result—increasingly lacking desire themselves. They find Drama Kings in denial of their own dependence on women—and ambivalent about women's diminished reliance on them. They find Drama Kings striking out in confusing and unforeseen ways; making cracks about how things have changed— how women are gold diggers, ball busters, tough bitches—but not talking openly about this "change" in a heartfelt manner. Strong women see these men advertising on Match.com and Nerve.com for women with PhDs—but also telling researchers that they want to marry "subordinate" women, their secretaries or their assistants, women whose job it is to focus exclusively on them. These women find Drama Kings accusing women of wanting too much while clearly wanting everything themselves.

These women find Drama Kings not only commitment phobic but also change phobic.

"These are guys who might as well write their ads like this," Aisha said. 'Wanted: Cooks, cleans, has her doctorate, makes love on command, makes a fortune—and never fails to remember to send out the birthday cards.'"

"It's not, 'Looking to *share* life,' " Kim added, "it's 'Looking to add new requirements of women to the old ones.' "

The women I've spoken with over the past three years are part of the country's growing force of strong women, and they are grappling with the new questions about love that are at the heart of this book. Some of the women are baby boomers who are back in the dating world after divorces; some are their daughters, dating for the first time. These young women came of age in the 1990s, one of the longest periods of job creation in our history, when half the graduating lawyers, more than half the doctors and veterinarians, and forty percent of business school graduates were women. Some women fall between the two generations—not married but in their late thirties, in and out of the dating world or on its periphery for twenty years.

The legacy of the Industrial Revolution has left all these women with the bulk of relationship management—the greater interest in and better tools for negotiating intimate relationships. But the impact of women's new double-barreled strength on their intimate relationships has left them and their potential mates in a bind. How does the high-achieving, self-confident woman in a demanding career make a man feel good when, for centuries, the answer was bound up in her availability, her selflessness, her obsession with pleasing? How does the powerful man in a demanding career make a strong woman feel good when the answer was for so long bound up in his ability to make money, his mandate to dominate, protect, and provide?

Drama Kings do not care to look at these questions, nor do they care to develop the kind of interpersonal strength they have lacked. They view the job of maintaining connection and encouraging cooperation, not to mention housework and childcare, as a necessary but low-status woman's job—not a "manly" labor and so not desirable to attain. Because they blame other factors—often feminism or women themselves—for their very real sense that they're losing power, stature, and control, they do not care to negotiate or compromise. They need and love strong women more than ever but simultaneously feel baffled and threatened by them. Their covert dependency on women, historically kept under wraps by both genders, has become more exposed now that women's overt dependency on men has lessened—and Drama Kings don't like it.

For the first time in history, women can create relationships to fit *them*, rather than having to fit themselves into a paradigm of love that's psychologically and emotionally crippling. They can choose a man not for safety, not to have a life, not for money and security, not to "earn" the love they crave, but for pleasure and companionship and fun. Drama Kings don't like this fact at all, don't want any part of this new paradigm—however beneficial it could be to them.

The strong women in this book, although awaiting transformed relationships with men they're eager to love, nevertheless at some point in their own transformation found themselves playing out a worn-out script with Drama Kings that implicitly denigrated their newfound status and hard-won attributes. For a while, they unwittingly and reflexively handed over their precious strength to these men, believing that in time, love itself would right the balance. Drama Kings, though, don't right balances.

But strong women do. Once the thrilling, sexy, maybe-this-is-it part ends, once the glamour and the possibility of an intimate relationship evaporates, the women I spoke with *got it*. It's not ambivalence, that familiar and normal push and pull of growing intimacy they felt from these men, it's an emotional heave-ho. Drama Kings, who want strong women—but who drain their energy, drive them insane, devour their love and their time, and leave them exhausted—no doubt have always done so. But now they're bearing witness to women's ever-growing resistance and resilience. I hope that this book helps strong women identify Drama Kings early, get what they need from them quickly, dispense with them gladly—and return to the richness of their lives joyfully. So they need never again feel that they must choose between feeling strong and being in an intimate relationship.

Chapter Three

Drama King #1: The Visitor

*If I hadn't married Tom, I wouldn't be as strong as I am now,
as wary of the signs of not being treated the way I want. These
intense tornados that I walk away from—though ridiculous,
embarrassing, uncomfortable—have taught me so much.*

—*Drew Barrymore, in* Harper's Bazaar

On Joanne's twenty-seventh birthday, friends kept exclaiming that
she looked great, so vibrant and flushed, until she finally admitted what was up. All their guesses were wrong. No, she wasn't
getting lovelier with every birthday, nor was she particularly
thriving after her divorce. It was not that she was still such a *wunderkind* at work or perfecting the art of motherhood. It wasn't even
that she was "in love."

She was getting it on with Fred.

Fred, the owner of a realty firm in Lenox, Massachusetts, was
her dream man. Her type. Not too tall; stocky. Thick, sandy brown
hair; blond hair on his forearms; nice hands—she always noticed
men's hands—and chocolate brown, soulful eyes. He was as familiar
to her as a brother—if she had had a brother—and the first time he

smiled at her and she smiled back, the deal was made. The deed was done exactly five hours later.

Afterward, he told stories about his clients—the ones buying the huge new homes, the McMansions, and the ones renting the tiny places deep in the mountains, funky little handmade homes that once housed members of struggling rock bands in the 1960s and still looked the same. He could tell the minute he met his clients, he said, which ones were going to "pan out." Then he spoke about his life: divorced parents, the father on his third wife; a sister on her third marriage at the age of thirty-three; a brother living somewhere in the Berkshires but unseen by Fred for five years. He told the stories deadpan, and she found him hilarious. How could you adore someone this quickly? Well, she did.

Fred came over to her house once or twice a week, a loose arrangement she fell into after that first time. "Maybe we'll see each other Wednesday?" he'd say as he was leaving. "If I'm through early enough. You wouldn't believe the couple who came in today." Okay, she'd say, hearing only the Wednesday part.

Maybe, he always said.

As literal as she was, and as eager for certainty as she was, too, she had trouble hearing that "maybe." All men, and women, too, seemed to start their sentences with "Maybe we'll . . ." these days, so she finally just mirrored them cheerfully, sometimes tacking on a mocking "*Whatever.*" At some point, after dozens of maybes had materialized, she asked him—almost more out of sociological curiosity than for a reading on his commitment level—whether he would consider them "a couple," and he smiled uncomfortably and said, "Maybe. But I guess I wish you hadn't asked that."

She wished it, too, because she'd found she rather liked their arrangement and didn't want to seem as if she were pushing for more when in fact, it was the ideal setup for her at this moment in her life. It wasn't too time-consuming. It didn't make her crazy or sick or distracted. It was different from what she knew and different from what she knew she would want some day. She eventually wanted a lover and a fulltime companion, but for now she was swamped with work as the head of her own insurance firm in Albany, and she literally couldn't afford to buckle under to pressure to choose between a career and a relationship. She was afraid she might choose the latter out of some atavistic reflex, and she truly didn't want to. She knew more would make her feel guilty because she didn't have more to give.

Their sex was amazing. She told him their bodies fit each other. Corny, she knew, but she had never nestled into a man so neatly; she had never felt that even her *skin* was happy next to his.

"You're great—I'd better watch out," Fred had told Joanne after their first night together.

"Watch out? Why?"

"I dunno. I guess 'cause I'm just not the dating type."

Who was, these days? Joanne didn't believe dating still existed, not in any recognizable way. What the hell was a "date," anyway? Who asked people out anymore? Joanne had noticed, she told me, that courtship was dead. "I've never really been asked out," she said. "Not technically, anyway, like where a man calls you up and says, 'Would you like to have dinner with me next Saturday night?'"

Fred is a Visitor, and Visitors have been around for a long time. They're classics, vintage Drama Kings. Their appeal is growing in direct proportion to the number of women who feel they're too busy to devote much time to an intimate relationship. Because these women are unavailable themselves, Visitors' lack of availability suits them. Visitors fly in a few times a month from abroad, or they check in from the neighboring state; wherever they live, though, they're not around much. Strong women who get involved with Visitors often overlook great guys nearby who haven't yet heard that dating is passé.

Joanne, briefly married in the '90s, now wanted her freedom, not to "play the field," as her parents used to say, but to pursue her own interests and do her work. She saw herself now as one of "the elder stateswomen of the hooking-up and hanging-out generation." Any woman of earlier times, before the death of courtship, wouldn't recognize what men and women did now, she said.

We all just sort of merge if the feeling's right at that moment, and then if we do and keep it up for a while, we get really tight as friends and then morph from friendship into sleeping together a little more regularly. And then . . . like . . .

Yawning theatrically, as though stultified by the boredom of the ambivalence, the imprecision of the language, the vagueness of the plans, Joanna went on to say that this arrangement suited her fine for now. She liked hanging out at her house in Lenox, takeout Chinese, *Desperate Housewives*, and sex with Fred. Fred always commented on the fact that *women* seemed more promiscuous than men. "All those wives sleeping around," he'd say, with the unspoken coda, "If only I could get at them!" She and Fred would have a real dinner sometimes—one of them would cook chicken or pasta *puttanesca*, and then they'd watch the news and make love. He'd leave early in the morning.

For all the irregularity of this arrangement, nobody had ever made Joanne feel better in bed than Fred. Out of bed, though, between visits, she found herself becoming oddly agitated. After about six months, she began to feel that there was something *too* abrupt about his comings and goings; something *too* casual about their dynamic. She didn't want more of him, exactly, but she wanted something more out of the times they were together. Despite seeing each other for six months, each time he left, she felt as though the relationship were being severed permanently. It didn't feel ongoing; it was as though she had dreamed the sexual connection between them. He was as amicable as could be when he showed up, but he made it clear that when he didn't show up, he wasn't to be questioned. Nor did he question her. There existed a feeling between them, she said, that they were meeting for the first time each time they saw each other. No "How was your meeting last week?" or "What did you do over the weekend?"

Joanne referred to Fred as her "guest" because he acted like one. He came and went but never settled in—physically or emotionally. In fact, when she expected him, she put out hand towels and little soaps and shampoos she'd filched from the Four Seasons Los Angeles when she was last there, hoping the little L'Occitaine touches would please him but knowing, really, that there wasn't much chance of that. He wouldn't notice; like any visitor, he just expected a working bathroom.

Things were fine, but only in the way that going nowhere is ever fine. Even when women like Joanne begin these relationships thinking things are "just fine," they find themselves admitting to feeling wistful for something more involving. If it were a loving relationship—a reciprocally loving relationship, that is—they'd be less unnerved. They'd know problems of all sorts were part of the deal; they'd feel they were working things out. But these arrangements feel one-way, unreciprocal, *unrequited*. Some other story—with a slightly less flighty hero—is in their bones. Something with more continuity, more affection. Joanne was confused because, while she didn't want the old story, the conventional one that featured marriage right away, this story, however freeing, was slightly bizarre in its motionlessness.

She took her PDA out of her handbag and did some calculations.

I began dating—it was still called dating then—at sixteen. This means I've been dating fifteen years of my life. When I figure it out, that means roughly 750 dates, if we assume Saturday nights only—close to 4,000 hours, or 166 full days and nights in a row, if you put the hours all together—with men I didn't know and might not even have liked.

Joanne hated this calculation. It made her realize how sad it was that mating was no longer synonymous with dating and that both were devoid of courtship, with its long, elegant history and clear-cut rules, its mesmerizing love stories of Mr. Darcy and Elizabeth Bennet, Mr. Willoughby and Marianne. For better or worse, these cautionary tales of romance and ruination had become a part of her brain tissue, and their observations about money, manners, and morals were still darting in and out of her consciousness.

It was in these moments when Fred was away, or she was on a business trip—and she had no idea when they would get together again—that she wondered why Mr. Right, a man so vivid in the old story that lived within her, was so *not there* in her life. She wanted, if nothing else, to have a conversation with her lover while she was in Chicago and he was wherever he was.

I'm not looking for a man, still. I don't need him. But I want someone in my life—who is in my life. Not a hookup, not a hangout; not a cell phone or e-mail buddy or someone whose picture I shot on my PDA-slash-camera-slash phone. A—dare I say it?—relationship. Someone I can call and who calls me. Regularly. On time. As promised. Someone who wants me as I want him—does that make sense?

She didn't know if she was hopelessly old-fashioned, with her desires for some systematic plan for coming together with a man.

For Joanne, as for so many women in her position, the old and the new felt utterly irreconcilable, and she didn't know which she preferred.

> *It doesn't have to resemble courtship, what I'm looking for, with the prescribed happily-ever-after ending. But how 'bout an occasional bona fide date, like with a plan for dinner or the theater? Being in the moment is a fine thing, but it could have a . . . a mindfulness. A sense that an evening together is chosen on purpose, not just fallen into because you both found yourselves on the same block and had nothing else pressing to do for the next hour or two.*
>
> *I'm thirty-one years old, and I'm hanging out the way kids do in college dorms—that alone is weird. But what's weirder is, as a grownup woman, I wonder about grownup values. Really. What happened to sexual exclusivity? To permanence? To forever? I mean, I know that we live longer now, and the idea of forever is so different from what it was when life spans were, I don't know, forty years, and I know no one stays in a relationship forever anymore. But is "forever" dead?*

How do you move forward with a man who not only has no interest in the courtship but whose very traits feed into its death? The Visitor has transformed the unstructured but sexual nature of *hooking up* into an art form, incorporating the lack of planned, structured activities into a ménage à deux. He is one of the architects of the death of dating, having helped render defunct the systematic forward motion implied in the word. Certainly, he will not make a concerted effort to make an evening, let alone a relationship, happen. He doesn't make a plan for fun. He has no strategy for moving a get-together into another get-together or a last meeting into the next. He has no scheme for developing intimacy, with its promise of moving into commitment, with its promise of becoming exclusive or even getting engaged to be married.

With such nonexistent initiative as the Visitor's, women who buy into this commitment-avoiding strategy can't help but find themselves asking the same question Joanne asked, in effect: What *is* this thing?

> *Look, I'm not saying I want to head toward marriage. I'm as ambivalent as he is about that. But I want a relationship that has a few elements of stability: namely, commitment, reliability, a story of its own. Something that is ours. Something about which we can say "we."*

Fred, like all Visitors, continued to come and go and never make himself fully at home. He checked in at Joanne's as though she ran a comfy little bed and breakfast, albeit one for which someone else is picking up the tab. When the plumbing was mucked up or the dishes needed doing, he looked at them, or her, like, "Oops! That needs attention!" But not from him. What he and most other Visitors want is to be assured of some sort of pleasure during their stay, usually sexual—but by no means anything that puts too much claim on their time or feelings. The Visitor is not looking to live there, after all.

Sunday was Joanne's most languorous day, at least theoretically. Fred often spent the morning with her after sleeping over on Saturday night.

One Sunday around 7 a.m., Joanne brought steaming cocoa

and caramel sticky buns to her lover, along with the paper. Fred, however, was doing jumping jacks next to the bed, preparatory to going out for a run. He was suddenly anxious, so much so that he mumbled something about knowing it was their only day together, but on the other hand, he had to take his run, feed his dog, phone his father, meditate, and do his taxes. In fact, it was the only day for the next month that he could clean out his garage. And write letters.

This happened so often that Joanne—who used to like to sleep in on Sundays but rose early to accommodate Fred—simply waved him on, assuring him that reading the Sunday paper alone would be pleasure enough. God knows she wouldn't chastise him for the bizarre list of made-up chores he had just come up with or bother asking, "Why don't we just not spend Saturday nights together?" For months, she had excused him for his lame list of chores by telling herself he wasn't ready for full commitment. She rationalized by saying to herself that, well, neither was she. But this time, she was humiliated enough that even she couldn't pretend any longer. Clearly, the idea of sleeping in together was so odious that he'd even lie if he had to in order to get back home.

She was right, of course. He *didn't* want to spend more time with her. Her place was nice to visit, but he didn't want to hang there for very long. And he would always make sure Joanne got the message that he thought she was trying to domesticate him, to seduce him into being husband material, what with the steamed cocoa and the sticky buns. Like a sensitive owner of an inn, she actually began leaving the breakfast in the kitchen in a Ziploc bag, as if he had a plane to catch, rather than bringing it to bed.

"I should just go out for breakfast alone and not leave a note," Joanne said. "He'd approve of that, actually. But I can hear my mother's voice saying, 'Now, don't be rude, dear. You're too fine a person for that. He is a guest in your home, after all.'"

By the sixth month with Fred, Joanne's initial vibrancy changed into a kind of anxious fatigue, which, on top of her exhaustion from work, led her to wonder whether she should stop dating altogether for a bit. Her energy had never been a problem for her, but then again, she'd never before experienced this peculiar mood split—this abrupt swinging from in-bed adulation to out-of-bed isolation. The suddenness of the disconnection after the intensity of the bond was enervating and confusing. She wanted the sex, but she wanted her energy back more. Her career left little room for this drain.

Was disconnection a problem located in Fred? Or was her distress, her exhaustion, rather, *her* problem? Perhaps she was just too distracted by work, and she was projecting her own detachment onto him so that he was the one who *seemed* distracted. Or was she so unmodern, so uncool, that even though a relationship that didn't dominate her life was precisely what she had yearned for and had arranged for herself, she couldn't hack it—the straight-out sex, untinged with love, without a promise of tomorrow? Wasn't *connection* what turned a date into a relationship, what turned something chilly and mechanical into something warm and alive? Or was she reading from an old script? She really didn't know.

The second time he spent the night, Fred told her something that is a common Visitor utterance. Many Visitors will say right at this early point that they don't think they're ready for involvement. They can't ever see themselves marrying. They aren't sure they can commit to a woman—any woman, so don't take it personally. Love is too hard to do.

What Fred said was that Joanne was too good for him.

"You're right," she said.

"No, really," he said.

"Really," she said wearily.

Joanne knew all she needed to know right then but hid it from herself and him: Fred was not trying to get closer but instead was emphatically pulling back. He was not struggling to accommodate the new, crazy feelings brought on by intimacy but instead had a mechanism firmly in place for rejecting them and a plain announcement to inform her. *No, no, no.*

The Visitor is never looking for a soul mate ("or any mate" Joanne added. "He's looking to eat and run, if you'll pardon my language."). Obviously, the unfaithful married man is a famous Visitor, but it could be argued that he fits the type solely because of his situation, not necessarily his character. The Visitor is *characterologically* a guest, and even single, so-called available men are champions of the breed. Some Visitors actually have married, but usually only for expediency, such as to solve a Russian girl's complicated visa problem. They are temporary marriages, not to be confused with marriages that simply don't work out.

The fact that these men can then claim to have been married once gives them currency in the mating field they return to and fools future lovers into believing not only that love and attachment were involved but also that it could happen again. The stories they tell—about a Russian girl—add drama and complexity to the marriage and suggest promise of more intrigue for the next lucky beauty.

But it's no use. However sexy the story, the listener must read between the lines. The Visitor is a loner. He learned early that one way to a woman's heart is through her genitals and that once he got there, she would want him to stay. This—to be asked to stay, to be wanted—is both his need and his desire but also his greatest terror, the situation he can't abide. He may be a physicist or a pharmacist or a psychiatrist, but oddly enough, in his heart, seductive as he is, the Visitor prides himself on being a lonesome outlaw. Typically, the Visitor has one or two other women besides his main one at any given moment—for refuge, he tells himself. He thinks of himself as faithful in his fashion, with casual infidelity being a quaint luxury he allows himself—and anyone else, really—although sadly, he is often so expert at lovemaking that most women don't want anyone else.

He also may show signs of the kind of low-grade, if not clinical, depression for which he might never, ever seek help but which could account for his obvious social withdrawal, disinterest in many activities, and reduced talkativeness. If so, the difficulty of breaking through to him and making him want to connect is that much greater and not something the average woman can take on without help. Unfortunately, she will not have sufficient clout to insist on it. This is how he is, he says—never knowing that this is how he is *when seriously depressed.* Occasionally, a Visitor will become physically ill—develop a condition for which he must seek help—and only then be introduced to his need for therapy or antidepressant medication. And then, finding his distancing mechanisms no longer useful, the Visitor may leave the ranks of Drama Kings altogether.

A man this detached can often have a uniquely perverse effect on strong women, making them *want* him to stay even more. "It's like in high school, " Joanne said thoughtfully, "when a girl goes through this need to prove to someone who's unkind and doesn't like her that she's the greatest and decides, Dammit, he *will like me!* It's one of the saddest games girls play. *Let me prove to you that I'm lovable. Let me show you I'm the one for you.* It never works. He inevitably goes off with some hellish creature who is so mean to him that he's thrilled.

"So here I was, doing it at age twenty-seven," she said. "Pathetic."

Significantly, a woman involved with a Visitor often starts to act like one herself, coming and going and not accounting for her whereabouts, no longer inclined to ask him about his own comings and goings. In a defensive if lifesaving maneuver, she begins to pull away as dramatically as he. Said one woman: "I'd make plans with friends or get tickets for the theater by myself. This upset him, not because he was hurt but because it was such a change from my usual behavior. My treatment of him, mirroring his treatment of me, was of course defensive. I knew that, but I also knew it disabused him of his dearest, most deeply held fantasy: that as a woman I'm different from him and that my goal was to trap him."

He *needs* to feel that entrapment is just around the corner, which is why he developed his guest persona, his Visitor's mentality, in the first place. He needs to feel that while *he* may leave the door open to ending their "thing," as this man referred to their relationship, *she* wouldn't think of it. Seeing his own behavior mimicked steals his thunder and upsets the power balance.

And make no mistake, this *is* about power. Specifically, it's about "the power of the least interested"—an idea I've talked about for many years that I believe explains how it is that the Visitor, who always wins the least-interested award, always holds the power. He believes his nonchalance, vagueness, and detachment are what make him sexy, glamorous, and mysterious. This might not be a bad thing, if only his awareness led to insight; if only insight prevented him from abuse; if only he didn't have lack of interest so deeply etched into his character.

But Fred had all of the above traits. Joanne felt he never really liked her enough, got close enough to her, or wanted to be on the same wavelength long enough to see who she was. She felt he was too busy checking out and checking in, making and breaking plans, buying and losing cell phones, playing computer games and pool, looking at stock quotes, and living the chaotic life that effectively took up all his energy and time.

Whatever attachment needs he might have had were deeply buried, so the relationship never managed to gather steam beyond the first check-in. She tried to make it seem as if it had but knew this attempt at ongoing connection, a reflexive urge and wishful thinking, was a mockery.

> *There was narcissism on my part, too, or maybe just ego. I be-*
> *lieved I could make him care about me, even though he'd made*
> *statements like, "I don't know if I'm capable of loving." I'd be like,*
> *"Oh, yeah? Just watch! Let me have at it!"*
>
> *Once, when we actually went to his place, I called him when*
> *I got home. "Just wanted you to know I made it home okay!" I*
> *said reassuringly, as if I were calling my mom or someone who ac-*
> *tually cared whether I got home okay. Thus prompted, he said,*
> *"Great!" even though it was obvious that the thought of whether*
> *I got home safely or not had never occurred to him — he didn't*
> *even feel caught or try to cover himself with a "I was about to call*
> *and check, but I thought I'd wait till I took a shower." I was filled*
> *with shame. For trying so desperately. For having to pretend*
> *so hard that this man was interested in me that I actually*
> *attempted, without being conscious of it, to instill in him old-*
> *fashioned good manners or ancient gallantry — how Victorian*
> *is that?*

This is a man at whose place a woman dare not leave even the most insignificant possessions, lest she seem to be quietly, stealthily, encroaching on his space.

> *I once left some things of mine in Fred's bathroom. Now you*
> *know that some men would have loved that, loved the slow,*
> *growing intimacy of it; enjoyed the actual physical evidence of*
> *becoming a couple. Some men would have stored the things for*
> *me, tucked them happily inside a drawer that would be designated*
> *my drawer.*

Not Fred. The next time he came over to my place, he brought with him the pitiful items, the miniature toothbrush and toothpaste from an old American Airlines giveaway, in a large Ziploc bag! He handed it to me, saying, "Hey, you must have missed this stuff," but what I clearly understood was that he didn't want anything of mine in his home. Again, I felt that rush of shame. I could hear my neighbor Bobby saying, "Joanne, why don't you take your little baggie full of dental floss and get the hell out of this insulting setup for good and find yourself a nice man?"

But do you know what I did instead? I confronted *him. I said, "Oh, my stuff! Gee, Fred,* thanks! *But hey, is it really a problem for you to have my toothbrush in your medicine chest? We do, after all, occasionally have sex at your place, and a few niceties there wouldn't* crowd *the joint, now, would they?"*

And you know what he said? He thought a moment and said, "Well, no, not crowd it exactly,"—I should have left right then—"but we're not living together." That's it. We're not living together.

"You're so right," I said right back to him. "We're not!" And then, before my sarcasm went out of control, I shifted gears and decided to try to understand his position. I used a validating technique. "So what you're saying is, I shouldn't leave a toothbrush at your house because we're not living together. Have I got that right?"

I had, evidently, because there was no further discussion. He nodded, is all. I tried the next step, which was "Did I get it all?" and he nodded again. "And is there anything more you'd like to say about it?" A "Nope" nod. So I didn't go on with it, and he didn't even try to cover himself with kind excuses—"My mother always told me that until I got married, I shouldn't share my space," or whatever. Just . . . nothing. A wan but topic-terminating smile that all but announced, "I don't want to go there."

In one further, truly pitiful attempt, with that stupid baggie he handed me in my murderous hands, I ran upstairs and found one sock of his in my laundry . . . just one unwashed Thorlo men's tennis sock, and presented it to him. "You may need this," I said as I handed it over.

"Thanks," he said. "I was wondering where it was."

Why I didn't take a knife to his throat, I'll never know. But at least I didn't try to justify his lack of connection, his lack of feeling, his obtuseness, his mean-spiritedness any longer. And thank goodness I didn't decide it was my mission to change him. And instead of talking myself out of seeing his schizoid behavior as an issue ("Not a problem," I'd have said before, in the days when I was into endless accommodation. "No big deal!"), I finally got the fact that he wasn't all that interested.

So, instead of telling myself that it was a good thing that we weren't enmeshed like new couples sometimes are; a good thing that I was a busy woman and he was the perfect undemanding adjunct to my life at this moment; a good thing because I didn't want anything too close right now and blah blah blah, I got it— and told him very politely not to stop by again.

I held my own. I stopped the game of trying, trying, and was willing to walk—or, to be precise, let him walk.

Years ago, eminent marriage therapist and researcher John Gottman, PhD, began observing the body language of men and women he was treating and observing, too, the change over time in their dynamic. In one film, a couple was sitting next to each other, with the woman leaning in to try to explain herself and to connect and reach out, and the man, her partner, sitting back in his chair, arms folded across his chest. He wasn't listening, or else he didn't want to or couldn't or wouldn't respond. In subsequent sessions, one could observe the woman trying less hard, not leaning in so much, with defeat, anger, and resignation evident in her hunched shoulders and facial expression. It appeard to me that once the woman gave up—started rolling her eyes at her partner's recalcitrance or simply stopped leaning in, not pushing for interaction—the relationship was over. *Finito.* She was through.

A strong woman can't both defer to the Visitor and stick to her guns. Joanne, as a strong woman, chose to stick to her guns. But she still had doubts.

> *I was proud of myself and sure of my decision and certain, finally, that I didn't want him. But I still wonder, sometimes, if I'd stuck it out—just waited—would he have someday come around? Was he just waiting to grow up?*

Her questions lie at the heart of women's dilemma now, a dilemma handed down like an heirloom from their mothers, grand-mothers, and great-grandmothers: Should a woman wait? There are old-fashioned, hard-to-get games to play; famous methods for turning reluctant bachelors into loving suitors. The change in women today, though, is profound: The specter of accommodation and silence, of scheming, faking, and insincerity, leaves them with an overwhelming sense of unfairness and palpable, undisguised anger. Compliance of this sort, the strong fist of self-betrayal, hits them in the belly. But they also remember the ancient techniques used for centuries by women to take the hit. Deference, selflessness, "handling" a man, can sometimes feel as if it's the *only* way to defend oneself and make headway. How else to make a dent in an object as immovable as patriarchy itself, now embodied in the Visitor?

Women are desperately tired of the game, but occasionally, when honesty and forthrightness fail, they see no way other than "influence" to budge him.

Joanne's defense mechanism, denial, declared Fred's insensitivity, stonewalling, and insults "no big deal." Her denial was self-betrayal, she knew, but it obscured, for a time, the pain of his disinterest. Going back to her fantasy of winning him by waiting him out, she said:

> *Holding my own would have meant having to say so many things: Expressing my true feelings about his cluelessness, his rudeness, his inability to connect, his profound ambivalence about me. How do you go into all that with someone who truly doesn't have any interest in the relationship? You just become a shrew. I mean, this man is out the door already, even in the good times. I should have just been ready to leave long before I did. But I wasn't strong yet; I still felt that old primitive fear of letting go.*

Woody Allen once said a relationship is like a shark: It either moves forward or it dies. With the Visitor, though, it does neither. It just treads water, seemingly hovering on the brink of becoming something but never paddling closer to what one could even call a loving friendship. Joanne mourns that fact. "It's the endless nondate," she says.

"It doesn't deepen or turn into anything more. That's 'forever,' all right, but only in the form of my worst nightmare. Forever going nowhere. What it was on day 1, it is on day 200."

Joanne's wishful thinking had propelled it forward in her mind, added depth to it because of the growing comfort with each other's body. But in her heart she knew the truth. While the sex seemed to suggest a forward motion, Fred could have gone on forever, unmoved, immovable. For him, it was a comfortable routine, like hanging out at a good old diner in town where you know the menu and like the waitress and see no reason to get your morning coffee anywhere else.

For many women who have escaped tumultuous relationships, a man like Fred can at first be a welcome relief. He makes so few demands.

"Here I was, thinking, 'Now this is a lovely, laidback fellow,' " said Susannah, CEO of a large California computer-game software firm. "Nothing freaky about him; nothing invasive. In fact, Justin wanted to know so little about me that at first it was a relief. No 'What do you do?' or even 'What's your sign?' on our first meeting. No attempt at even the most clichéd of connection attempts. He didn't care. You know, I don't think in the year we went out, he ever asked when my birthday was . . . but I knew *his* was September 14th from the third time he came over."

Again, it's that powerful phenomenon, the one I see so often that comes up in so many circumstances: the power of the least interested. Often, women remember the little things—a man's birthday, fantasies, favorite foods, important relatives and events— from the moment they hear them for the first time. They are . . . interested! How ironic that this interest can put them at instant risk for seeming *too* interested; how sad that interest poses any disad- vantage whatsoever! How disheartening that women are obliged to rein in their natural instinct to connect, to relate, to remember, lest they appear to be too interested—and so they relinquish their re- lationship power *because of* their relational strength!

Perhaps this is one reason men aren't eager to develop rela- tional strength with women: Instinctively, they know that their power has long lain in keeping distanced from all that detail, that focus on family dynamics, the keeping track of birthdays and the caring for day-to-day minutiae that keep love and relationships alive. They know well that the person who labors for love occupies a lesser position than the one who works elsewhere at loftier things. Out in the world, where men's strength has long prevailed, "power" meant power *over* someone else, and to them, that's what it must mean at home, too.

Justin's power over Susannah didn't feel stifling, so she thought it didn't exist. "He adored my independence—never cared what I did, where I went, who I was with," she says. "It was both freeing and horrifying. I think if I'd told him over dinner, 'I had four lovers today. Want another piece of pizza?' he'd have said, 'Really? Wow, awesome. Sure. That big piece there, with the extra cheese.'"

Susannah's vacation from intensity soon began to feel like Siberian exile because her emotional needs went so unmet, her power to connect with Justin got so thwarted, and her individuality—who she is and what she believes, thinks, knows, desires—was clearly, as she put it, "profoundly irrelevant" to him.

Scholars have long been interested in the different ways women and men speak to one another. We know by now that women ask more questions and say "you know," much more often than do men. But in a study called "What Do Couples Talk about When They're Alone?" Pamela M. Fishman attempted "to understand how power relations between men and women are reflected and maintained in everyday conversation." Her interest was in finding out who is more likely to get a topic moving in a conversation, and her findings, drawn from men and women between the ages of twenty-five and thirty-five, are haunting. Raising a topic is an attempt to produce conversation, and Fishman found that many of women's attempts to initiate topics failed, while none of the men's did.

Women raise *so many more topics than the men because so many of their topical attempts fail. The failure of the women's topics is not due to their content, which is often indistinguishable from men's.* The failure is due to the failure of the men to respond, *to work at turning the attempt into a developing conversation [emphasis added]. Women use a number of interactional strategies to try to increase their chances of success, strategies that men seldom have to use.*

Women ask questions nearly three times as often as men. Fishman explains, "This is not out of insecurity. Questions ensure that you will at least get an answer." They say, "D'ya know what?" more often than men. "Here, one not only ensures an answer, but the answer, 'What?' is another question which invites the first speaker to continue." And the women in this study also used the phrase "you know" ten times more often than the men did. "Their uses of this phrase are not randomly scattered, however. They increase as the men give minimal response more frequently or stop responding altogether," Fishman states, adding that these devices, which seem to be female, are not. "The few times that men have difficulty maintaining conversation, they use the same sorts of devices to get attention and response. But women have much more difficulty getting conversations to succeed than men do, so the strategies appear to be female ones."

One of the most fascinating aspects of this study concerns the cliché that women are needier than men are. "Women *seem* to need more attention than men do because they must often work harder to get it in conversation. Men *seem* to not need attention because they get it with very little effort," Fishman observes.

Susannah said that sex was the only relational language Justin spoke; other forms of intimate communication made him uncomfortable. The specific form his discomfort inevitably took, she noticed, was disinterest and hostility, and it most often manifested as paranoia.

> *Because he was always on the lookout for entrapment and was unable to envision intimacy as anything other than my secret plot to drag him into some kind of torturous permanence, he watched me so carefully for signs that I might be presumptuous enough to foresee any future contact with him. We never made dates in advance. He always waited till he was out the door before saying something vague like, "See ya!" or "Catch ya later."*

Sound familiar? I had the impulse to put Susannah and Joanne in a room together. Their Visitors might have been the same man, except for their names.

The Visitor, whether Fred or Justin or anyone else, comes to all conversations with the fear of being trapped, manipulated, caught out. He is so convinced that the woman comes to believe it herself. He never lets down his guard, and all conversations about love, friendship, the future, traveling, even having dinner next Saturday, will elicit his assumption that he's in danger. Nothing his woman says is, to him, casual, impulsive, or spontaneous; it is directed, disguised, or plotted. Similarly, nothing he says is casual, impulsive, or spontaneous; it is coming from a rigid psychic position—that of someone who doesn't trust her.

It's often said that women express many of their feelings in order to have them validated; men want to fix things. Strong women's relational style is indeed to connect—and to these men (whose impulse is *not* to fix things), that feels like being tied. Strong women tend to seek connection in words, in time—asking intimate questions to assure intimacy, making plans to assure continuity. To these men, this feels like tripping onto a bear trap.

Try it, if you ever want to see the Visitor's paranoia blossom: *Mention a future event.* Go ahead, suggest a plan—having dinner with your sister, a drink next Tuesday, even a scheduled phone call—and witness uniquely bizarre distress. It's as if you've said, "So, Justin, let's get married on Tuesday, have a huge, expensive wedding!" or "Fred, let's have seven kids together!" Your actual words, "Pizza later in the week?" or "Tennis Friday?" will prove just as frightening to him. ("He won't say no," Joanne said, "but he'll cower in the background and fiddle with his cell phone. 'Mmm,' he'll mumble amiably, but his whole body language will have changed. He'll fidget. He'll go jogging. Anything . . . to shut out the horrible possibility of making an actual plan.")

Because exchanging information also makes a connection—like having each other's personal trinkets in your pockets—women often ask for personal information. "So Justin, what did you feel when your father left home? Weren't you just nine years old?" Susannah asked Justin, thereby "convincing him that I was trying to psychoanalyze him," she said. "And that meant that I was surreptitiously moving in for the kill, wanting to own him. I can't tell you how many times I had to tell the guy that I didn't want to marry him. I didn't."

She didn't. What she did want was:

Something like what we had, but with less fear attached to it. A man who, whether he wanted to be committed forever or not, was committed to now enough to be present. Isn't that what mindfulness is? Being in the moment? Believe me, I could be very happy that way. I'm truly not looking for more. I already have two kids. I have no need for a husband, and I'm not sure I want to marry again. I'm not even sure I'm against serial monogamy, as Margaret Mead suggested, or even non-monogamy. But theory aside, for now, I'd like a partner. A companion. A friend. Someone to play with. Who doesn't poison all interaction because he thinks I'm trying to snare him.

With Justin, it was a terrible game of "gotcha!" Were it not for his extraordinary lovemaking abilities, Susannah would recognize Justin as just your garden-variety Peter Pan, a boy-man who wants to fly but not connect. But because he was so adult in bed, she hadn't dubbed him thus. He had a genuine talent, an instinct, for sex—the way other men have a genius for playing the clarinet or making cabinets. Joanne, too, had convinced herself that the arrangement with a lover who was always halfway out the door worked for her. She herself knew what it felt like to be a Visitor, during those times when she was working too hard, and she knew what it was like to put one's career first. She believed, deep down, that a more nurturing man, with more of a nesting instinct, someone who wanted to live with her rather than check in occasionally, would want more of her than she could give.

What she didn't understand for months was that she was already giving more than she had to give to the Visitor and that a more nurturing man wouldn't make her feel, as she put it, "drained dry" and exhausted but instead appreciated and desired.

So, out of a temporary, pragmatic postponement of commitment, a strong woman becomes attached to a man whose fear of commitment is far deeper than her own.

Telltale Signs of the Visitor

1. He reveals himself quickly. Other Drama Kings have mastered the art of pretense. Not so the Visitor: He sends a clear message on or around the very first time you meet—the trouble is, you don't believe him. He says things that sound so much like clichéd boy-jokes that they're even cute, which unfortunately diverts your attention long enough to disregard the unamusing message. Remember Fred's words?

"You're great—I'd better watch out."

And Joanne's response? "Watch out? Why?"

"Oh, I dunno. I guess 'cause I'm just not the dating type."

This was conveniently heard as, "I'm more serious than a mere dating type," or "I hate *dating around*," or "You're the kind of woman a man gets serious about." Joanne, not the "dating type" either, thought, "Me, too! Dating sucks! You agree! Terrific!"

Earth to Joanne: Not being the "dating type" does not mean he dislikes dating around, it only means he dislikes courtship, like an event where he's expected to pay or to make a dinner reservation. Always remember: The Visitor feels his most generous act is showing up. Too, not being the "dating type" could well mean he's so promiscuous that he's never dated at all; he's therefore completely unfamiliar with what one does on a real, live date. (On one episode of the TV show *Huff,* the sleazy but brilliant Visitor lawyer played by Oliver Platt takes a woman from his firm out on a date. In the middle of dinner, he becomes so ill—not from the food but from the fact that he's on a date—that he excuses himself hastily and leaves.)

Not being the "dating type," in other words, doesn't mean he's looking for a deeply connected relationship; it means he's not. It means neither that he's better one-on-one nor that he prefers being in love. Not being the "dating type" doesn't find him by a fire with a glass of Pinot Noir, with you and you alone. No—all that coziness makes him a little sick.

2. He cannot tolerate intimacy. He experiences closeness as overstimulating, volcanic. To protect against being overwhelmed, and against the emotional failure he expects of himself, his strategy—to show up for sex but not stay long enough for intimacy—has a predictable outcome: mutual avoidance. You will hunger for connection. His behavior says, "I guess I have to get some contact with women, but I don't like to go out with them." Which is why he doesn't. He goes to their place. "Intimate relationships are not for me" is always in his mind, which is why when he leaves, you have no sense of whether he's coming back, or when. Even when the sex is terrific, you're never quite sure that he's not having that same good sex with someone else.

3. He counts on women to fill in his blanks. This is a man who knows, perhaps unconsciously, that many women will find charm in his vagueness, challenge in his elusiveness, because it feels like a break from all that aggressive, in-your-face testosterone they encounter. And so he uses a weird kind of flattery as bait.

Remember Fred's "You're too good for me, y'know that?" It was such a familiar line, so sweet, that Joanne took the bait.

"You're right," she countered, as if he were issuing a cool compliment, when he was actually being serious and honest. Other versions of this same message, such as "I don't really know if I can love," and "I'm not the marrying kind," are equally serious and honest but are oddly seductive to strong women because they're so tempting to prove wrong. They take it as a challenge. "Of course you can!" they want to say. "Of course you are!"

But his words aren't said in the middle of a soul-baring discussion; they're said at the door, as he's taking his shoes off and is about to dive into the meal you've provided. That they're being uttered at the get-go means they should be read as a warning.

4. He seems to be asking for help. His words sound beseeching—"Maybe you can help me with my buried desire to love?"—but in fact, if you listen carefully, they're not. The appropriate response is not "No problem, you cute thing, I can!" but rather "No, sorry, I think for that one you should get professional help." Or, at the very least, "No, sorry, not until that request is made outright and we become so committed to one another that it's worth my while."

Do not be tempted to interpret or analyze the Visitor. Do not be the Woman Who Understands Too Much. That's why we're not analyzing him right here—we could, if we wanted to be "good" women and not strong women, and if we wanted to spend time torturing ourselves over why he tortures you. But we aren't analyzing him because it's a time-consuming, thankless, unproductive role that only elicits scorn and disdain from Drama Kings. So just believe him. When he says early on, "I've had okay relationships," that's what they've been: A big yawn, just like yours will be with him soon enough. And do not think this tepid response to love was some woman's fault. When he says wistfully, "I don't really think I can love," you are not to fall into the trap of becoming competitive with past girlfriends; you're not to read it as "I like companionship but haven't found the right companion."

Never, never, never, never take the position that you're going to show a grown man how to love. Particularly not a Drama King—and specifically not the Visitor! You're not equipped to release his rage, to excavate his ambivalence, to heal his profoundest wounds. To take on such a task is delusional. The hackneyed script he lives by—the withholding wanderer and the welcoming savior—is nothing more than a dark cautionary tale. The strong woman should hear nothing but "WARNING! I DON'T DO LOVE. I MEAN IT. AND IF YOU THINK YOU'RE DIFFERENT AND TRY TO MAKE ME CHANGE, I'LL HATE YOU AND BLAME YOU AND PUNISH YOU."

5. He doesn't participate—in anything. He's interested in his car, not yours. His breaks down? It gets to the shop. Yours breaks down? Good luck to you. By extrapolation from his lack of interest in you, you can figure that your stuff is nothing for him to care about, either. That means, no kitchen help, no laundry help, no help at all. Certainly no help with expenses. You'll notice this right away, and it's kind of chilling. He doesn't pitch in, really; he just sort of looks around vaguely when dinner is being made and sometimes even looks edgy, like, "When will this be served?" He's not interested in your mother, your kids, your ill grandmother, your broken stairs, your scary medical report. "Oh, really?" he says distractedly when you bring up events in your life. They're yours to worry about. Get it? He's worried about what's on the dessert menu and whether you have a restaurant-quality cappuccino machine.

6. The Married Visitor—I shouldn't have to tell you this—*always* has a sad story, usually about his terrible wife. When a Married Visitor says, "My wife and I don't get along very well," or "She and I don't sleep together anymore," and yet he still goes home to her, you know not to buy into it, *right?* To the disappointed man and his horrible, sexless bitch of a wife? All you need to hear from his sorry story is "I'M MARRIED AND LIVING AT HOME." The heroine of the story is the strong woman. But guess what? The strong woman is not you, it's his wife, sexless bitch that she may or may not be. The ending? A tired old story. He will visit you every Tuesday or Thursday. Don't even *think* of weekends.

Myths about the Visitor

There's only one myth: *He just hasn't found the right woman yet.*

True, but you are not that woman. And you don't want to be. Here's why.

The disconnection that he illustrates so clearly took place long ago, between the ages of three and five, when boys are taught to be strong little guys and to be more like their daddies than like their sensitive, feeling moms. But all that tenderness and feeling in him, the "feminine" part of him that the boy so suddenly disowned (and disdained) in order to join the company of men, stays inside him in the form of an intense sensitivity that women see and tenderly protect. I have called this protection of men's sweetness, tenderness, and vulnerability the Protection Racket—not to be unsympathetic but because it's a terrible arrangement for both genders. For it's a woman's knowledge and compassion—remember that "compassion" means "to suffer *with*"—that are called upon to heal a man's wounds, but *secretly* called upon, so he doesn't feel that which he's spent a lifetime suppressing. I bring up this psychological truth not for the purpose of analyzing him—I promised I wouldn't do that— but to show the tenacity of the Visitor's skittishness. He doesn't want an arrangement that renders him so dependent, but he doesn't want to change the arrangement either, so he darts in and out of it.

Strong women, however, do want to change that arrangement. That's why they have worked so hard to boycott the old deal that asked them to "earn" love through self-sacrifice the way one might earn the Purple Heart in the military or sainthood in the church. This covenant requires both parties, though. Getting the Visitor to want, let alone attempt, increased relational responsibility is impossible without *his* willingness, *his* involvement, *his* commitment to the process of coming together. Without that—and he's denied you that—there *is* no coming together.

Why You Were Taken In

Because you needed to learn about boundaries (everyone does), and in this case, very strict, impermeable boundaries. You were struggling to understand the difference between the lover who is noninvasive—who gives you enough space to have your own life—

and the lover who offers space at the price of connection; who is neither involved in your life nor inviting you into his. You can't learn this subtlety without going through it.

What You Learned from Him

It is the lesson of the century: *to hear the story that's being told, not the one with the fantasy ending.* Strong women may be tempted to make up romantic endings because that's what women used to do, were even encouraged to do, and wanted to do—but we must learn to guard against or even deny this succubus. We must believe that a grown man knows himself better than any woman who just met him ever could. Hear him; don't rewrite his sentences. He has said, over and again, in every possible configuration, "I like companionship once in a while, *but nothing deeper.*" He has said, in every way, that the boundaries he needs are big as the outdoors, and that's a space that leaves you out in the cold. He has openly provided every possible clue to the outcome of your relationship.

Chapter Four

Drama King #2: The Proprietor

There is only one big thing—desire. And before it,
when it is big, all is little.

—*Willa Cather*, Song of the Lark

I don't think I've met an experienced woman who has been in the mating game for even a short time who hasn't come across the Proprietor. There's something profoundly appealing about this aggressively attentive lover, because he appears to be a true, old-fashioned suitor. Women refer to him as "very *male*." In a world of ambivalence, ambiguity, commitment phobia, and vagueness, he appears on the scene like a welcome blast from an earlier era. A woman who meets up with him after tangling with the Visitor would think, "Here is the perfect antidote."

Phoebe was an attorney at a law firm in Charlotte, North Carolina, where her brilliance had made her a partner within ten years—the only woman to become one, and an Asian American woman at that. She was working on a campaign against a major clothing design firm accused of outsourcing jobs that should have been held by Americans. She'd been through two "bizarre" relationships in the past two years. You wouldn't have guessed it; she didn't look haggard but rather young, happy, and calm at thirty-seven—as if the aftermath of these bizarre relationships infused her with a lovely and peaceful strength. She even said as much—she never felt herself to be a victim of these relationships. She had wanted them and had learned a thing or two. Now that they were over, she felt blessed. Best of all, she was no longer afraid of her own complicated, contradictory, confounding emotions in her love affairs, no longer surprised that they occur in a jumble or that the men in her life don't understand them. But she had recently fallen deeply for a Proprietor—and for the amazing sex they shared.

Good sex, Phoebe had concluded after experiencing both fiery and more tepid liaisons, comes with involvement. "Eye-to-eye intensity, that's for me," she said, "which pretty much eliminates all that hooking-up-and-hanging-out fucking" that you get if you're free. Real intimacy took away that neediness, she said, "that feels like lust but has a desperate tinge to it because you're thinking, 'Oh, no, I'm letting go here, and he's just withholding.'" Desire, at least for Phoebe, needed "reciprocity and intensity" for it to be fulfilled.

Peter was nothing if not intensely desirous of her. When she met him, it was "instant combustion," she said. "I fell in love the minute we sat down at the restaurant." He was neither distracted nor casual but focused, aggressive, and attentive. He remembered everything she said to him. He noticed what she wore, who her friends were, what she said on the phone to others while he was in the room. He loved her looks, he told her, and her clothes—declaring them "simple, elegant, a little stark." Like *me*, she thought proudly. The man was all alertness and vigor. He seemed to generate heat in the air around him, as if energy molecules were furiously pulsing in his aura. Whether that energy of his would ultimately distort the space around him or just fill it with warmth, she didn't know, but he couldn't be ignored.

Nor did he ignore Phoebe. Not since high school, when she'd soared ahead of the boys in everything from mathematics to basketball, had she received such scrutiny from the male gender. When Peter asked a question, he'd search her eyes, back and forth, like someone doing an acting exercise in developing eye contact or, she later came to believe, as though looking for evidence of something. Evidence of what, she didn't know. Meanwhile, she was enthralled.

The main focus of Peter's relentless attention was lovemaking. He displayed such an unerring, unflagging sensitivity to every one of Phoebe's physical sensations that she couldn't believe her fabulous good luck. "He was better sexually than anyone else, in any circumstance, ever," Phoebe said pensively. "He had unbelievable concentration. His mind never wavered; he was totally, uncannily, into me.

"He was also focused on being a *couple*," she said wryly, recalling the wavering attention spans of more desultory Drama Kings in her life (she, too, had been with a particularly skittish version of the Visitor, just before she met Peter) and found this newfound attention "heaven" by comparison. This, she thought, is what it's like to be consumed; what intimate sex is supposed to be. "Everything that came before it was too ambivalent and intellectualized, too neurotic and fearful and uncommitted. This was go-for-it, I-want-you-and-you-alone, man-woman stuff at its most primitive and unquestioning." She was reminded of those insects that get stunned by their predator before being eaten alive. For the moment, she was happy to be in its thrall.

This was sex like I couldn't believe—and I hate to admit it because it's racist and a cliché, but I never thought a white guy could be so amazing in bed. Peter was sensitive, but so alert to any perceived shift in the content of the conversation and in my attitude toward him that I was afraid to say anything casual, for even the breeziest of comments was closely attended. "What did you mean by that?" was his motto, and his face would darken if I so much as commented appreciatively on what he was wearing.

Whereas the Visitor in her life had noticed nothing, followed up on nothing, cared about nothing that was said other than what time he should come over, Peter cared about every word, every gesture. At least, he cared about what pertained to him—what he perceived as being his business: Who called and who's coming over and who said what when.

"He particularly wanted to know what I said—to anybody," Phoebe said. "He wanted far more than just to check in." She laughed as if remembering something. "He wanted to own the joint."

This sort of scared me. I had so much work; I was so stressed. My son, Scott, was growing up so fast. It never occurred to me that I was in danger, though. I was a tough lawyer, by my own and others' standards, and here I was with an artist. [Peter was a painter.] I loved it. And I adored giving up all that protective armor I'd built up. I felt freed—just giving in. Why? Because we were soul mates. I told him everything about me, and he told me everything about him. I've never been so close to anyone in my life.

Look, I'm in a tough field, a world where people chew up and spew each other out all day long. Here's this romantic, attentive guy, planning special weekends for me. I love literature, so suddenly I'd be whisked off to a poetry reading, a Shakespeare festival. He'd find out which museums were having shows I'd love, then he'd go to great trouble to find a nearby hotel that he knew would please me. And the sex—oh, God. We'd play games, play out our fantasies, talk dirty.

He paid such attention to me. I don't know how else to put it. The other two important men in my life before him literally never paid attention to what I wanted. I know that sounds strange, but it was as if they both thought they knew; considered themselves such accomplished lovers that I was incidental. They both had a routine *down pat, some weird set of motions they'd learned with someone else—in high school? With previous girlfriends? From a book? I never knew—but by George, whether those motions suited me or not, ain't nothin' that was gonna change those twirly movements on my breasts, that mechanical up-and-down motion on my clitoris. If I moved their hands to show the pressure or motion I actually liked, it didn't take. The next time, there would be the same old routine again. Such an immature, reflexive kind of sex, so much about their ego and their fundamental disinterest, makes you feel as used as a teenage girl in the back of a car. But Peter's sensitivity was lovemaking at its most extraordinary.*

I'd been awakened as if from a coma. I'd always heard about feeling a sense of oneness but thought I'd only find it in yoga! This was a religious experience. He wasn't afraid of my strength. He wasn't terrified of my sexuality. He wanted more, more; he wanted me to go crazy with desire, and I did. He'd whisper things like, "We were destined to be together," and "No one could ever love you the way I do," and "We've only begun; wait till you see what comes next." It was laughable at first—it was so primitive, this man who makes all other men, no matter how loving, seem commitment phobic by comparison.

Some women would feel smothered in this hothouse environment, but it was what she'd always craved, and once Peter sensed this, he made his move. He cleverly started to take possession physically, emotionally, and psychologically. Now, Phoebe was not easily owned. She was used to being self-sufficient, in control of herself and her son and even her parents, whom she supported emotionally and financially. Everyone depended on her, and no one fooled around with her. Or so she thought.

But suddenly, Peter, also divorced and with two children of his own, Georgia, eleven, and Petey, thirteen, who lived with their mother in Wyoming, had become the owner not only of the relationship but also of Phoebe's soul. And her son, seven-year-old Scott—who tried to please Peter but clearly hated him—knew it. "Why do you let him bully you, Mommy?" he'd ask. Phoebe would think, "I can't help myself, my child: The sex is too good. The connection too explosive."

> *"He's not bullying me, Darling," I'd lie. But Scottie knew that Peter had begun to control my time. Scottie became clingy—something I'm embarrassed to admit because I know why children become clingy. My friends were a little appalled, thought Peter was a psycho. But to me it all seemed innocuous, so . . . male, and maybe even if obsessional, I'd handle it. I wasn't concerned. I was too strong a woman to be controlled by anyone, let alone someone who loved me. I thought it would all calm down.*
>
> *But then came the growing barrage of questions. "Who's that on the phone?" he'd ask. "Don't you think your mother is a little too . . . involved with you?" and "Why do you suppose you look at other men all the time?" and "You're really going out in that skirt?" and "Funny that you hired a male secretary, don't you think? What's the real reason, do you suppose?"*

Significantly, these questions occurred, at first, right after sex—when the phone rang or when Phoebe got up to bathe or when she'd run off to feed or play with Scott or drop him off at school.

The Proprietor rages at such interruptions, resents them, takes them personally. The very liveliness and sexuality that he adores in his lover becomes a threat to him within a nanosecond after her attention moves away from him.

He got mad at her for everything. He implored her to work on her "problems" ("of which," she said, "I apparently had legion") so that he could "continue to love her." She was a "controller," he told her, and pointed out every action on her part that proved it: flirting with someone in the store, trying to push him into taking a vacation, angling to get her mother to come over, always trying to change him. Her good points, as dissected by him, soon became bad points: Her friendliness was "promiscuousness," her dedication to work "fear of relationship," and her beauty, well, it made her "too slutty." She learned from him that she lacked the "feminine" capacity for closeness and commitment, for domesticity and childrearing. "You're kidding," she said, pointing to Scott as her shining example of her domestic and childrearing skill. He said, well, yeah, but she didn't know how to handle a man. *That* was what he meant.

He was the kind of man who talked about "real men" and "real women," and damned if it didn't all sound like something out of Oklahoma! *except that anyone who wasn't a "real man" was a man he wanted nothing to do with, and anyone who wasn't a "real woman"—which meant all my friends and, increasingly, me—he belittled, as though we should be somehow "set straight," another of his terms, about the "real" working of the sexes.*

I teased him and cajoled him to drop his stupid, redneck worldview that was so embarrassing to me, so wrongheaded and humiliating and misogynistic at its core. After a while, I lost my original indulgence toward him and instead became nervous about pulling away from him after making love or having my nipples show through a sweater. "Are you wearing a bra?" he'd ask before I went to work.

I can't believe I put up with this shit. It would be so incredibly good, so unbelievably close, and then, boom! *I'd hear this grave, accusing voice, like something out of "Sinners in the Hands of an Angry God": "Why do you think you need to go to the kitchen right now?" as if there were something horribly unnatural about being thirsty after two hours of sex and something questionable about my hunger for anything other than him. "'Cause I'm thirsty," I'd say cheerfully, "and I thought you might be, too."*

He'd simmer for a while, throw out more questions that insinuated that I was up to no good somehow — "Funny, you weren't thirsty fifteen minutes ago," — or mumble that I had no ability to retain closeness — and would stay annoyed until I came back into bed, moved once again into oblivion with him. Oh, and if a friend would call during all this? Forget it. He'd stomp around, leave. I had to take the phone off the hook whenever he was around.

In time, Phoebe says, Peter became enraged by any interest she had outside him, including Scott. The workings of the firm, the success of the case—not to mention her hobbies, her charities, her choir, her love of hiking and biking, to which she was able to devote only moments of time now—were to him outrageous diversionary tricks being played *on him.* Even her focus on Georgia and Petey, *his* kids, upset him.

Vacations with Peter, once dreamy sexual and romantic idylls, became a nightmare. I could only take a few days at a time away from the case, and often we'd bring Scott and sometimes Georgia and Petey, too. The kids got along fine most of the time, and the time away was precious to me. So there we'd be in a restaurant, and I'd be looking around while the waiter got our food, thinking, "Nice crowd; nice to be here," and suddenly I'd hear this low, pinched voice: "I see what you're doing."

And I would say, "And what's that?"

"I see you flirting with that man over there." And I'd look over at some guy behind Peter who I didn't even notice—I'm legally blind, you should know, even with my contacts—and I'd shrug. "I didn't even see him, you lunatic."

He'd go on, in this righteous tone: "And in front of the kids."

I took him aside privately, "You know, Peter, this is absurd, it's just absurd. You're ruining everything. You're scaring the children. And you're annoying the hell out of me." And he'd say, "You just can't control yourself, can you, Phoebe?"

And it would begin. His diatribe against me, this raging preacher. "Don't tell me you didn't see him; I saw your nipples get hard when you looked at him." It was crazy.

Now, this offended me. It was crass and disgusting and untrue.

One time we were on a wonderful weekend in Washington, D.C., and we were laughing and telling stories, and I remember telling one about my family, one that contained evidence of my having had a husband—I mean nothing overt, just a reference to the fact that I did at the time of the story have a husband, and he went ballistic. So the whole weekend, this marvelous weekend, turned into a nightmare, and he remembered it only as the time that I spoke about my ex-husband. I said, "Peter, I left him, for God's sake. We're divorced. Isn't that enough?"

No. He hated Phoebe's ex-husband and was afraid she didn't. He hated most of her friends, too, particularly the ones she loved most. Hated her family. Detested her past, made up scenarios about her future.

One day, Phoebe came back from lunch with a friend, and she'd also gone shopping.

> *"Strange," Peter said when I got home. "You said this morning you were going to be downtown all day. But aren't those packages from Nordstrom's?"*
>
> *"Yup; why?"*
>
> *"Isn't Nordstrom's in a different part of town?"*
>
> *"Yes it is, Peter. Why? Is that a problem, its being uptown and not downtown? Ever heard of cars?" I had changed my tune dramatically. Six months into this thing, and I was as sarcastic as he was accusing.*
>
> *"Funny that you didn't tell me, that's all."*
>
> *"Are you accusing me of lying? Please correct me if I'm wrong, but are you suggesting that I went someplace I really had no right to be going? Or is it that I shouldn't be buying myself something? Or that I shouldn't be buying Scott something? God knows I'm not spending your money, Peter, so which of these heinous crimes is it?"*
>
> *He wasn't even embarrassed; he just kept right on. "What time did you say you got there?"*

The Proprietor searches and searches for the one piece of evidence that will reveal for sure what he so clearly thinks he already knows, for the one indisputable fact—what time you got there, what time you left; when you said you'd be home, when you actually got home; how long it takes the bus to get to your stop and how long the walk is from there; whom you said you went with or sat next to—that will *nail* you. You see, the Proprietor has the answer to what you did, knows the sin you've committed; it's clear to him, and no evidence to the contrary can persuade him that he's wrong—only that he's right but doesn't yet have all the facts lined up to his satisfaction. Like a cow with its cud, he chews on his fantasies of betrayal slowly, slowly, never letting anything, including the truth, distract him.

He won't get off it, ever. He is paranoid. In the words of psychoanalyst David Shapiro, PhD, author of the classic book *Neurotic Styles*, the true paranoid personality is "peculiarly uninfluenceable and marked by special willfulness and tense, unrelenting purposiveness and self-direction." You will never dissuade him, in other words, for he will ruminate and obsess and persevere until the nonexistent evidence of your wrongdoing somehow materializes. Some Proprietors are equal-opportunity paranoids, attributing questionable motives to everyone. Others make only their lovers the bad guys.

Michaela, at forty-eight a widow with four children, was head designer for a women's clothing firm when she took over her late husband's charitable foundation. Swamped with work and family, she met a Proprietor named Carl, a wealthy businessman and the largest donor to her family's foundation. At first they merely worked together, but soon—a year after her husband's death—Carl began pursuing her urgently and showering her with gifts: diamond necklaces, cars, art. "It was like in a movie," she said, and while she was flattered, she waited another six months before beginning to go out with him. Once she did, he called her five or six times a day. She said the sex was "unbelievable; like nothing I'd ever experienced. It was nuts, all of it—me, a matron of fifty just out of mourning—but how could I give it up?" She said something similar to what Phoebe said about Peter.

> *There's something powerful in handing yourself over to love, to a lover, particularly when you sense that the person loves you so much and can't wait for you to give in, or rather give over. See, you read that as his being able to take you on without the usual fear men have. I know it goes against the thinking about strength, like, strong women wouldn't want to "give it all up" to someone—but that's victim stuff, and it's not true.*

It *is* strong to be free to give up your defenses. It *is* strong to trust. It *is* strong to put your heart into working things through. It *is* strong to be vulnerable in love.

Unless you're with a predator. And Michaela was. Carl was married, which he never told her, and she didn't find out until well after she was deeply sexually involved. She stopped seeing him.

> *I didn't see him for about seven months. I began casually seeing two men, both single, both lovely; then I got this phone call from one of Carl's friends: He'd been in a snowboarding accident and was near death and in some hospital in Canada and wanted more than anything in the world to see me. Would I please, please go to him? It sounded as if he'd had an epiphany, was about to announce one of those earth-shattering change-in-life plans. So Johnny-on-the-spot here rushed to his side.*
>
> *"You're keeping a secret from me," he said with a terrible, mean little smile the moment I got there.*
>
> *"What are you talking about, secrets?" I said. "I flew to Toronto to see you on what I heard was your deathbed, and you're going to accuse me of secrets? May I remind you of your little secret? The one about having a wife?"*

Damned if he didn't proceed to question me about my life, about dating. The man had tubes coming out of his nose and he was saying, "You're lying to me."

"I'm leaving," I said.

"What about this Joe guy I hear about?" It was like some-thing out of The Sopranos.

"Lying?" I said. "I'm seeing men who are free. You're the one who was lying. And how the hell are you getting this information anyway; are you having me followed?"

He smiled. "Don't trust your friends," he said.

"It's not my friends, Carl. It's you. It's you, lying here with four casts on, sending out your hit men to check on me. Am I right?"

"I can afford to be protected, if that's what you mean," he said.

As I was leaving, he said, "So what I wondered, Michaela honey, is, when this is over, can we go out again?"

Peter may not have had Phoebe trailed professionally, but he accused her of infidelity just as vehemently as Carl accused Michaela. And as constantly. As Phoebe said:

He could not assimilate the fact that I could be his best friend and also sexy. Like someone in a Victorian novel, I had to be a whore, *because how else could we be having the time of our lives in bed? . . . or a Madonna, because how else could I have such a great and happy child? It threw him that I was a combination of both, and I believe it was incomprehensible to him. I think he hated the strength and completeness of me. Really. He'd say, "Be* less." *I'd say "Less? Whatever for?" And he'd just scowl. Less what, you might wonder. Less everything.*

Every wonderful thing, every wonderful time, every wonderful sexual experience would become poisoned by this abrupt, psychotic decision that I was doing something harmful to him. He would get a look on his face. Mr. Hyde. As he said to me once, "When I walk in the door, I expect you to run up to me and give me a big hug."

And I would say, "Well, I'm thrilled to see you, but sometimes I just don't feel that—Scott might be doing his homework and need me the moment you walk in, for Heaven's sake. Get off it, will you?" I always thought a dose of reality would embarrass him, but it never did. He'd just say, "I don't care. That's what I want, and that's what I expect. And because you're such a strong woman, you're clearly not used to dealing with a real man. *Because a real woman would know all this, know how to respond to a real man."*

And what does a "real man" do for a woman in exchange for this unshakable devotion and demonstrativeness he expects?

Well, let's see. He shows up. And he has sex with her. And he happily admits his bias. He says, "Real men don't do anything else and shouldn't have to; now, where's that hug I asked for?"

But a Proprietor will never go for the docile "real women" he constantly talks about. He's desperately attracted to strength—and to the vibrant sexuality so bound up in it—but hell-bound to take it away. A strong woman's vitality, beauty, depth, and achievement all turn him on. But it's a little more complicated and a little less healthy than it appeared, for this particular Drama King is viciously jealous of that vitality, sexuality, achievement—and not only must upstage them with qualities of his own but must actually diminish them, somehow. He must take them away from her, tame her, control her. That's the thrill for him. But it's his downfall, too, and he reveals his underlying psychological need to push her away.

The Proprietor, the most overtly controlling of the five Drama Kings, is without exception attracted to strength, vitality, and high-spiritedness in women, like a hunter to a priceless jaguar, free in the wild. He loves it, wants it, craves it, desires it. The very vibrancy he's attracted to, though, is what he specifically needs to vanquish. His unconscious plan is built around trying to hunt down but then tame a glorious, spirited creature—not the "real woman" he idealizes, who is docile and accommodating—*and failing*. Failing, his deepest fear, is nevertheless crucial to his storyline, for it's the only plot he knows. It would be no fun for him, on the deepest level, to find someone who might easily bend to his will and *stay*. That would foil his self-fulfilling prophecy, which is that, try as he might, she abandons him. The drama lies in the shooting-himself-in-the-foot attempt to keep a sexual prize.

Obviously, a loyal, timid, mild-mannered girl won't do. He needs a strong woman. This is a compulsion, a repetition compulsion. As Freud said, one can never have a happy outcome unless one knows exactly what happened in the original drama, and why. Remember it, he said, or else be doomed to repeat it.

As Phoebe said:

> *I guess he knew he'd never keep me. But he kept trying desperately to control and change me. One time at a party, I expressed my opinion after some blowhard went on and on, saying that women really don't need to work, that most men make plenty for the whole family, and droning on about good mothers and good children, and of course I went crazy and asked what men was he talking about? What family was he talking about? Did his preposterous theory relate to the middle class in this country? Did it matter to him whether women wanted to work and needed to work or whether college costs $30,000 a year—or just whether he, a man, wanted control. . . . it was like something out of a*

dopey, dated country song in a redneck bar in the '80s. I said, "What world are you talking about? The world of single moms?"—and Peter turned on me. "You're full of horseshit," he said to me, and walked off with our host to go look at his pool room or something.

Terrified, the Proprietor now attempts to assassinate her character. Gravely, he presents his assessment of her deepest self: "I never realized how much your problems with your father created problems with being able to love a man." Darkly, he'll announce the reason for his bad mood: "I'm just beginning to see how your obsession with being a lawyer is a substitute for involvement in your real life." Meanly, he moves to devalue and hopefully end her closest friendships: "I can see why you were friends in college, but haven't you outgrown her?" It would be different if the Proprietor could just be honest and say, "Me, me, me! I need more, more, more," but he won't. *He* is never the problem. The problem is you, you, you.

You and your faithlessness. He needs to prove, and will—even if he's wrong—that his lover has another lover, somewhere across town, or at work, or on the net, or at Saks, or wherever. She has betrayed and is about to betray him always, and all he has to do is find the evidence. So she does begin to hide those side trips to department stores or that dash into a coffee shop, not only because it's none of his business, not only because it will become the gruesome, humiliating, demeaning, and embarrassing obsession over dinner, but also because she doesn't want to play into insanity games. Betrayal lurks everywhere for the Proprietor, and the one woman he "loves" more than anyone in the world—Phoebe, in this case—is the one person he believes to be betraying him.

So Phoebe, so frantically busy at work and at home that she thought it was hilarious that Peter could imagine she had time for a lunch, let alone a liaison, found herself nevertheless doing dumb things, like pretending that the guy in the shoe department was a woman just to avoid having to admit to being in the same room with another male. She knew it was deranged, but it was easier. She once called her mother and said, "Look, I know this is nuts, but will you pretend I was with you last night between seven and nine?" She explained:

> *You're still both so vulnerable and in love, and you think it's all because of that, so you go overboard to protect his feelings, his sensitivities and vulnerabilities. Because I'd never dealt with anyone like this, or anything like this, and had never been so in love, either, I tried so hard. Only slowly did I come to see it was more than an unconscious setup on his part, his raging, it was on a* schedule. *Every week — every seven days — he'd put a bomb in our soup. We'd get so close, say, on a Saturday. By that night, he couldn't take it, so he'd push us apart. And while we all have ways of subtly disengaging, his was brutal; he had to make me wrong,* bad, *in order to withdraw. By Sunday? He was in a rage.*

And his rage was all about her; what she did or didn't do or said or didn't say. No one has ever arrived at such mistaken conclusions so intelligently and thoroughly. The Proprietor is like a cartoon Sherlock Holmes, brilliantly getting the facts right but coming to preposterous conclusions. As Dr. Shapiro observes, "Acute, narrow attention that is rigidly directed toward certain evidence can extract it and can impose its own conclusions virtually anywhere. Thus, the suspicious person can be at the same time absolutely right in his perception and absolutely wrong in his judgment." Even when getting help, such a man will attempt to poison the therapeutic atmosphere, not just thinking treachery exists but ensuring that it does.

The Proprietor defends himself from processing new material that would inform him about the current case. He ascribes all of his own pernicious fantasies (that you want to betray him; that you're already betraying him; that you already did betray him) to *you*, disowns them as his own and cannot be disabused of them. Reality is meaningless. His projection makes him psychotic—makes him break off connection with the real world—yet he is so smart, so otherwise functional, that you're inclined to disbelieve the fact that he disbelieves *you*. So you keep trying to bring the truth into the picture, but he'll have none of it. Phoebe said:

> *I didn't know I was capable of feeling such murder, such rage. I found myself drinking much more to kind of blunt the reality; to get away from how bad it really was. I gained twenty pounds! No, thirty pounds! See? Even now I'm ashamed to admit the truth of this debacle! My mother, who never mentions weight, suggested I go to Weight Watchers when I hit 160 pounds—which was, she said sweetly, more than I weighed in the ninth month of my pregnancy! Peter was rather happy about it because God knows, nobody was looking at me! I looked like hell, I was disgusted and ashamed of myself, the sex wasn't worth it anymore; it was all too sick.*

Phoebe called the next example "the worst it got."

> *I had spoken at great length, maybe an hour, to one of my partners on the phone. When I got off, Peter said to me, "I'm taking the kids out of here, I will never come back, and I will never see you again, the way you've humiliated me in front of the children, flirting with this man." He got his stuff together and said, "We're going to stay tonight, but tomorrow I'm leaving."*
> *And I said, "Oh, no, you're not! You're going right now!" I*

started throwing all his things into a bag and said, "You are in my house, I'm making dinner for you and your children, and you're accusing me—and now you're going to stay over one more night because it's convenient for you? Get the hell out of here and don't come back. Ever."

But you know what I did? This is how sick I was, and I'm ashamed of this, but later, after this terrible scene, terrible and in front of the children—probably ruined their lives—you know what I did? Two days later, I called the man, the other lawyer, a very close friend of mine who knew Peter because we'd socialized, and asked him to call Peter. "Just tell him that there's nothing between us," I said.

He said, "Phoebe, I'll do this, but you do realize that this is over for you two, don't you? That this is . . . not cool, if this is what's going on?" And I persisted, "Please, you know him, you know me, just call him." Which he did! And Peter called three days later and said, "Gee, thanks, Phoebe, now you've made me too humiliated to face the guy again."

Yeah, and I cannot believe, to this day, what I did.

Some people don't believe strong women have moments of acting not so strong. Their fantasy is a prototype of perfect psychological health, as though strong women walk away from bad behavior the moment it occurs or never get involved with men who behave badly in the first place. Ah, would that it were so. No, strong women are not clairvoyant. They cannot spot a bad situation they've never been in before (although they do learn from it). And they're certainly not inured to the craziness of relationships. As agents of their own pleasure, though, strong women don't become mired in that craziness. Not for long, anyway.

By then it was over for Peter and Phoebe, and she knew it was over. Here's how she got out.

Some old friend of his, a gallery owner in Vancouver, offered to give Peter a show. He'd actually been painting pretty well for a while—big, angry-looking installations made with bent steel and sheetrock—and couldn't wait to show them. He begged me to come with him. I was frantically busy at work, of course, so I couldn't have even if I'd wanted to. And I didn't want to: I wanted out, although I didn't say so directly because frankly, I couldn't handle another scene.

He knew I was happy not to go and, being who he was, knew it was the end. But instead of talking about it openly, he did his thing: He began hinting that I had an "unnatural" relationship with my mother, whatever that means.

"Are you suggesting I'm having an affair with my mother? That I'm an incestuous lesbian? Is that it now?" He just looked at me with a kind of "Well, you said it, I didn't" smug expression, and I said, "You are ungodly."

I began unloading. I can fight like the lawyer that I am— I'm told I'm scary—and I went after him with the same meticulous violence with which he attacked me, only I analyzed his motives to show him how sick he was. I remembered every fact of his life, and I used his sexual history to prove he was projecting when he accused me of infidelity. I knew the names of every woman and man who'd come on to him—because he'd told me— and I began to show him exactly how much he wanted to fuck them and then how he disavowed that desire and placed it onto me, and that projection was the origin of all his psychotic fantasies; that they were displaced. I went wild; played Psychotic Analyst to his Psychotic Boyfriend, in a kind of "If I can't beat him, I'll join him" maneuver.

I became equally as disgusting as he. "Why do you always get yourself involved with gay guys?" I once asked, going for his "real

*man" thing. "You always need people to kiss your ass? Is that it?"
I wanted to disarm and humiliate him the way he'd disarmed and
humiliated me. I gave up my agenda to prove myself, even protect myself, and dropped the good-girl stuff and just went for the
jugular in any way I knew how. And I found, to my horror and
delight, that I was great at it, this vicious game of his. That I
wasn't afraid. That got to him.*

*So here's my Pyrrhic victory: I betrayed him just as he be-
trayed me. His self-fulfilling prophecy that I would leave him
came true.*

*When he left for Canada a week after he first heard about
the show, I changed the lock on my door so fast he'd barely reached
the car when the locksmith arrived.*

For other women, getting out is not so easy. Proprietors do
not go away. Like squatters settling on a piece of land, they do not
disappear. They stay and stay and stay, no matter how terrible the
relationship.

They will tell you this thing you have together is "love." That
no one will ever love you as much. That you will be sorry. In this
way, as in others, they are often scary: There's so clearly the potential for trouble—for stalking, for rage—since that kind of trouble
lurked so often in their "loving" interactions long before the
prospect of a breakup. Proprietors rarely leave on their own, and
even if they stomp off in a huff and vow that you'll be sorry, that
you'll never see them again, that you've really done it this time,
they return when their desire for you overwhelms their pride—in
a few days. Remember, their attachment issue isn't avoidance; it's
the need to merge. They'd as soon stay forever and torture you as
leave and be all alone.

"Me! Strong woman personified!" said Samantha, a math scholar and professor at MIT. "Look up 'strong woman' in the women's studies or academic literature and you'll find *me*: African American, single mom, PhD." But her own profoundly effective power was no match for a Proprietor, whose major strength is his ability to drain strong women of theirs.

Hell if I wasn't becoming the dumbest, weakest girl in town with this asshole. I was lying to him and to myself—and to everyone else. But still seeing him. Till finally I became ill, physically sick, like a woman imprisoned in some horrible tenement situation, like I'd inhaled too much asbestos or eaten too much plaster. My best friend, Dana, came over one day, looked me straight in the eye, and said, "I'm serious, Sam," and handed me a domestic violence pamphlet!

"Oh, please," I said to her, like, hey, it's not that bad.

"Yes, it is. And don't you dare *not take this seriously," she said. She was shaking. Her lips were ashen. "Don't you dare continue lying to yourself like this." She was pointing her finger at me, about two inches away from my face, and her face, well, I'd never seen her enraged before. "And don't you* dare *blow me off like this. READ IT." So I promised I would.*

"Now," she said. "In front of me. Out loud."

It listed the things that qualify as abuse—controlling your time, isolating you from friends and relatives, the list we all know—and Liam was guilty of every one of them, including tracking my time and cutting me off from my dad and stepmom, who I'm very close to. He always claimed to have a good reason— "You need to spend more time on your work; stop frittering away your time," and "Your mother is draining you; you've got to put your foot down or you're going to be giving up your life to her."

Dana was right. She was a godsend, because I knew it but didn't know it, if you know what I mean. Didn't want to know it. That old trick of denial and self-betrayal: putting aside what you know in your heart in order to beat the odds, or beat your family's pathology, or win what you've never won before . . . whatever. The big lie.

Pathological jealousy "explains" many of the yearly two million cases of wife abuse that come to public attention in this country. It is provoked by nothing except the demons that live in the disturbed man's head and by his tragic lack of compassion for the woman he wrongly blames for his inability to keep those demons at bay. Regardless of the shame at its core, the results can be deadly for the women who are jealousy's victims. Any strength they thought they had is siphoned off by their love for the guy, their sympathy for his plight, and by the Protection Racket I mentioned earlier. Women who have been smashed in the face for not being home "on time" or scalded for not having heated the soup "properly"—or verbally abused for not being "real women"—are closer to the fires of hell than the strong women at a party who are accused by their Drama Kings of "coming on" to their dinner partners—but only by a few degrees.

Samantha recalled the incident, two months after her talk with Dana, that pushed her out. It embarrassed her, this scene, because it was so wildly out of control that she couldn't believe it happened to her. She couldn't believe, that is, that her strength had been so depleted that it got to this point.

Liam and I were at a party in Boston, and we were sitting around a dinner table, all leaning forward, and my arm was grazing Jim's arm—my friend's husband—while I was speaking. I looked over and I saw this expression on Liam's face—a twisted, ghostly expression, the grim reaper look, and I sat back up. "We'd better go," he said solemnly. I marched out like someone in a school for wayward girls, and he said, in the car, "You know, you are really a slut. How can you live with yourself?"

That evening, when we got home, as he was going on and on, I took out a knife and held it up to his throat, and I said, "One more word about me and you're dead. Now get the hell out of here and don't ever, ever come back." He left, with his usual, "Don't call me telling me how sorry you are; this time, you've done it. I'm not coming back." Like leaving was his idea.

In the past, he could wait me out. This time, all I thought was, "I came close to murder." I have it in me—no problem; I could have stabbed that man—and you could be interviewing me in jail right now. And that motherfucker would be all over town saying, "Poor Samantha; I never realized how sick she was," with some other fabulously strong woman on his arm.

Samantha, Phoebe, and Michaela weren't physically abused by their Proprietors, but they were lucky. Said Phoebe:

Because it became such a volatile relationship, I made it clear to Peter that if he ever touched me, I'd call the police. So, no, it never became physically abusive, but it was so verbally abusive that I told him I didn't trust him. Didn't trust him—after all that nonsense about trusting me. He changed, wasn't verbally abusive anymore, but the damage was already done. I had told him everything, and he had betrayed me, and it was over.

One Proprietor I know came to a party of mine not long ago— as the companion of a strong, funny, and talented woman I care about very much.

They arrived, Francesca and Paul, holding hands, and they kept holding hands even while having their champagne cocktails, even while having a sit-down dinner. They didn't disentangle their respective fingers unless buttering their bread or cutting into their steaks. At around 10 p.m., when guests moved into the living room to hang out for a while, they actually separated long enough to speak with other guests. Francesca talked to Don, an actor, and Paul to Dina, a psychiatrist, and her husband, Jonas, also a psychiatrist. At about midnight, the party broke up, and everyone went home.

At two in the morning, my phone rang. It was Francesca, weeping. Paul had spent an hour yelling at her about her "betrayal" of him; her "lengthy" and "seductive" conversation with that "sonofabitch" actor, accusing her of being an incorrigible tease. "I saw how you looked at each other," he told her. "It was disgusting." "What are you talking about?" she asked. "He's a famous actor. I asked him about his life."

Paul then threw one of her Tiffany candlesticks at a lamp, breaking both and skimming the side of her head, and stomped out.

"I could hear it take a piece of my skin off as it whizzed by," Francesca said disbelievingly. "I had to get five stitches."

Next time, if statistics are correct, it will hit her right in the eye. And then it will get increasingly more violent.

The event left Francesca so nervous, so vulnerable, so out of tune with herself and her usual good judgment about men. She is horrified that she had entered a land in which she repeatedly denied what she knew: that Paul was violent.

Normal jealousy is not an emotion that just lies there ready to spring, bounding up to seize your lover every few days or so with still more "proof" of your provocative behavior, impending infidelity, or heartless betrayal. Normal jealous feelings are like a bad meal in a good restaurant—occasional. Digestible. A human response to legitimate threat. Abnormal, pathological jealousy is more like food poisoning—it emerges out of nowhere, toxic enough to make you ill, and seems to last forever. It dominates the relationship yet becomes so much a part of it that the very woman it compromises comes to accept it as a "normal" part of her life, part of her man, part of her future. Leaving the dynamic requires extraordinary strength. Maureen said about her Proprietor, who happened to be her husband:

> I thought I was strong when I got a divorce from my husband. I mean, I was able to maintain a household, raise a child, go to work, keep smiling. Actually, I couldn't get over how much I was accomplishing.—"I'm indestructible; I can't be beaten down."
>
> Or so I thought. The funny thing is that as resourceful as I am in life, most areas of my life, I came close to being beaten down. That was a huge shock. And getting away from my husband took every ounce of strength I had: I realized I was fighting for my life.

Of all the Drama Kings, I believe the Proprietor may be the hardest to leave. For a woman unfamiliar with jealousy, it feels like a sign of passionate love, something akin to the fatherly protectiveness many of us crave in a man. Of all the Drama Kings, he most dramatically triggers those old, deep, good-woman yearnings in us: namely, the impulse to prove our fidelity to him, to prove that we will neither hurt nor leave him. What we can't know until we learn it is the ferocity of his desire to shoot himself in the foot. He doesn't just think we'll leave him, *he's intent upon our doing so.* The good news is that so many of us do, and the world is a different place once we have experienced firsthand the difference between being dearly loved, which we had hoped for, and being invaded. I've never met a strong woman who has looked twice at another Proprietor once she has left one.

Telltale Signs of the Proprietor

1. **He is aggressive—but hypersensitive.** Although the Proprietor can have oodles of charm, his heavy intensity is palpable enough to distort the space around him. You feel that intensity in the air, feel that he *wants* you. At the same time, there's a skittishness to his desire, not an outright aggressiveness—what he really wants is for you to want him, and he's watching for your response. You feel an immediate responsibility to not hurt his feelings—as well as an immediate responsibility to explain yourself. He's so tense. Soon, you're walking on eggshells and don't quite know why. The reason is that he's hypersensitive to the normal movement of your attention. He refuses to believe you want him. You wish, in your heart, he'd back off a bit, but he keeps moving forward with all that vigilance and sensitivity. You don't know how to get him to calm down, to back off, to give you some room.

2. **Your men friends will like the Proprietor; your women friends won't.** I want to ask, *what* men friends? Do you have any left that he "allows" you to see? It's odd: Something about the Proprietor appeals to men (that "real man" thing, perhaps), just as something primitive in him is quieted, or reassured, in the company of other men—other men, that is, of whom he's not jealous. Your women friends will have a different response. Either they'll pick up on his gloominess and ready anger, or they'll witness a moment of intense jealousy on his part, a black cloud forming over his head, that will scare them. Even at the beginning, they will say things to you like, "Honey, isn't he a little possessive?" and "Sweetie, he wasn't so happy at the party the other night," and you will find yourself entering the Protection Racket by defending him. "He's very intense," you'll say. "He was just feeling a little . . . threatened." You will actually wonder if they're a little jealous because he's so sexually attractive.

Myths about the Proprietor

1. He is paranoid because he loves you so much. I can't say it often enough. Many women unused to Drama Kings feel flattered when a man is so jealous he threatens to break the knees of anyone who looks their way, but flattery it ain't. This kind of jealousy is insulting and shames you; it has as little to do with love as rape has to do with desire. (Who else who "loves" you would insist you're a cheat and a tramp?) Rather, it has to do with a host of other problems, from impulse control to overentitlement to serious psychological disorders. Even if he does love you, he feels he has the right to manipulate your conduct (and your mind) in order to compensate for his desperate fear of loss. What loss? Well, the loss of you, but also a loss that took place years and years before.

The wound to the young boy that I discussed earlier shows up again here. It shows up with all Drama Kings, but most obviously with the Proprietor. One sees how the early disconnection from his mother, forced on him in the name of becoming a "real man," left in him the scars from losing his greatest love, the true "real woman" in his life—his mom. One sees, too, how defended against this loss he became in order to join other "real men." You are being punished not only because of his old losses and the losses he foresees but also because of the stunted emotional and relational growth left in their wake.

My concern here, though, is that *you* not have to absorb the grandiosity and possessiveness, the anger and relational incompetence, your Drama King was left with. Yes, he's a victim, but you needn't be *his* victim, nor his unbidden savior. The loss he experienced years before he met you, but will forever blame you for anyway, is one that he doesn't have a grip on. Nor does he have a grip on the shame, the probable depression, left in the wake of lost connection. The most compassionate expert on abuse I know,

Steven Stosny, PhD, in a stunning speech at the Smart Marriage conference in Dallas in 2004, referred to men who may not be outright abusers but are "hidden" abusers as "blame addictive." He says, "They get up in the morning and think about what victims they are."

If he hasn't figured out by this time (with a good therapist) that his rages are not your problem and not a relationship problem but, as Dr. Stosny puts it, "a self-regulation problem," your only job is to run like hell. You could hurl your own and every other woman's love into that enormous pit of insecurity and shame called Peter or Liam or Carl, and he would still blame you, you, you.

2. Anyone as jealous as the Proprietor must be completely faithful. Au contraire. His jealousy is a projection, which means his feelings are projected onto you as if you were the one feeling them. What feelings? His own unconscious desires to betray you.

He shows an odd variation on the Golden Rule: "Don't do unto me what I'm imagining doing unto you," which is why his jealousy so often seems to be coming out of nowhere. It's not nowhere, it's just nowhere in *you*. This interpretation is used by analysts to help an excessively jealous person see that unfaithful feelings reside in his own head. Even so, and even if the same feelings were to reside in yours, neither one of you intends to act them out. Feelings aren't facts. Fantasies can and do remain fantasies.

3. As soon as he learns to trust you, his jealousy will go away. Alas, it won't. It will get worse, this lack of trust, the more he takes possession. The strongest women make the weakest mistakes when they think that sufficient love, commitment, and time will "prove" to the Proprietor that there's no need for jealousy. They also make the same mistakes when they believe, as Phoebe did, that the Proprietor is genuinely interested—either in them or in changing his behavior. In reality, he's not the least bit interested in you except as someone whose job it is to fix, help, support, complete him—the way a "real woman," wherever and whoever she may be, would. The Proprietor cares about only one thing: the fact that he's going to be hurt. The worst mistake is to think that once you are "his"—i.e., married, engaged, living together—you can prove to him that he won't be hurt. He will only begin spouting things like "No wife of mine will . . ." and "A real woman wouldn't . . ." The more you try to prove, the more there will be to prove. You can't prove him wrong, and you will inevitably prove him right because finally, you will leave.

4. It's best not to rile him up; just let him think he's right. No, don't. That's a weak woman's tactic and has no place in a strong woman's life. To give in, jolly him, or indulge him in this craziness plays into the abuse pattern with what's called learned helplessness. Learned helplessness begins when you think you're calming him down and taking the high road by ignoring his dumb charges, but you're doing neither. Instead, you're mistakenly assuming that his freaky possessiveness is rational, avoidable, and preventable—that anything from a good meal to a backrub will keep him sane. Welcome: You are glimpsing the world of the battered woman.

The bottom line is that the more passive you are, the more victimized you will become. Deal with his unwarranted jealousy actively and surely: "This is your problem, not mine. I refuse to accept your false accusations by dealing with them one by one and watching you ruin our relationship: Go get serious help and work it out without me." (By the way, anyone who's watched *The Sopranos* knows that narcissistic Proprietors become as suspicious of their therapists as they do of their lovers. They often leave therapy in a huff long before any good comes of it. Narcissists are difficult to treat because of their inclination to idealize, then debase, their therapists—much as they idealize, then debase, you.)

5. He is just a scared little boy. Rubbish. This is the lie women used to repeat to each other—"Men are just babies"—when they were forced to stay with Drama Kings. But men are *not* just babies. Mature, caring men who are all grown up, inside and out, are out there waiting for you—so don't sell yourself, and men, short with old saws like this one. And the Proprietor isn't a baby, either; he's a tyrannical, narcissistic bully. No one for a strong woman even to go *near*, because he craves her strength, wants it, and will take it. (When a woman says, "No man can destroy me; I'm too strong for that," take a look at a woman who's spent, oh, five years with a Proprietor, and see what she has to say then. Then notice how unrecognizable she is from the woman she was before she met him. Ask her about her self-esteem.)

Oh, and this "scared little boy" has one other quirk: He likes to have vicious fights and then to kiss and make up. What is it that makes him able to hurl his fantasied infidelity accusations at you—leaving you breathless with the injustice of it, your heart pounding with fury—and then be ready to seal the fight with a kiss? The same thing that apparently gives him the right to decide that twenty minutes after a fight, you must make love to him or forever go down in history as a withholding bitch who perpetuates arguments, carries grudges, and hates men.

Of all the exercises in male power, this—"Let's have sex and make up"—is the most insidious. What is presented as a loving solution to an argument—making love—is nothing less than a form of psychological rape (unless you happen to like the solution at that moment, too). It violates your needs in favor of his. It reduces your anger to a willful personality flaw that must be bullied out of you. And he will call all this control on his part "making up."

No, what he wants is not to make up but for you to "make nice." It's part of the "real woman" thing—cover-up behavior that doesn't correspond to authentic emotion. Making up is an unpredictable process involving the unique rhythms of two normal lovers, two separate people with different feelings, sometimes requiring three hours of conversation, two hours of weeping, four days of weirdness between the two before one says, "Let's watch *Six Feet Under*," the other agrees, and the fight is over. Sometimes you'll think you're ready, and you'll reach out to him and feel a surge of anger again and know the fight isn't over yet. And while making love can work it out sometimes, it has to be because both of you feel like doing so.

Making nice has been a strategy of the weak since the beginning of time, evident in animals who turn belly up when a predator is around. In humans, it requires that a nightmare of unpleasant feeling be buried under a gooey icing of politeness and cordiality. It's not compassion ("to suffer *with*") because it's not empathic, it's fearful. And there's neither compassion nor empathy nor mutuality on his end. Rather, it's a way to control you by controlling the course of your anger. He expects you to make nice; otherwise, he stomps out.

Squelched anger and sex make strange bedfellows. If you get past foreplay without breaking out in hives, you'll likely find your senses deadened, resulting in the need to fake orgasms—and there you have it, the *classic* make-nice technique of women who came centuries before you and hadn't a quarter of your physical, mental, or emotional strength.

Why You Were Taken In

Passion, intensity, and sex, for starters. He also seemed protective; nurturing; and very, very interested in you. All very good reasons, just very bad results. Loving is a behavior, not just a statement. Loving is as loving does.

What You Learned from Him

Passion, intensity, sexual thrill! And surrender—how daring it felt to let go, to be exposed. And what it feels like to be controlled, mistrusted, even disliked, by the person who claims he loves you more than anyone else ever has or will.

You learned what it's like to be nervous every time you go home, knowing that you're gonna git it for *something* you did or didn't do that day.

You learned that there's no causal connection between your behavior and his storms and that you can knock yourself out for someone and still be derided or even raged at. In your search for a man who isn't ambivalent, you learned what it felt like to be invaded. In your search for a man who wants you and you alone, you learned what it felt like to be psychically, if not physically, violated and possessed—virtually imprisoned. You learned firsthand the nature of the tragedy of loss—his, historically; yours, now—and must congratulate yourself daily for not staying long enough for it to turn into true tragedy (think *Othello*. Not him, though, but Desdemona.) Yes, this is a man you could have loved forever—had he not been hell-bent on ruining his own life and yours—and so you've learned the greatest lesson of all: Never to seek love from an enemy.

Chapter Five

Drama King #3: The Easygoing Guy (EGG)

There is nothing that gives more assurance than a mask.

—*Colette*, My Apprenticeship

For a man famous for his steamy political ad campaigns, Edward's laid-back, low-key style was a surprise to everyone who met him. His firm was the hottest in Dallas, and there was no doubt about his high-powered business sense. It was just that his style, his affect, was deceptive.

Bess was the segment producer of a Dallas morning news show. She met Edward at her television agency, and their business relationship developed into weekly strategy breakfasts aimed at pushing her show. Funny, offbeat, artistic, Edward had immense charm: "Hugh *and* Cary Grant charm," Bess said. He was appealing, big and demonstrative, she said, the kind of man who gives you a big handshake or hug when he greets you. Yet, away from work, he

97

showed none of the aggressive traits associated with being so busy and high powered.

"He was a couch potato outside work," she said, not disapprovingly. "A puppy."

Her colleagues revered him, as did his. Even her eight-year-old daughter, Nancy, declared him "cute, Mommy" when he came over the first time, and she began to ask when he was coming over again. She got a kick out of the possibility that her high-energy mom and this laid-back Texan with the drawl might become an item. Of course, Bess wasn't used to this, being the less cute and charming one, but she didn't mind. She was in the presence of a true winner— a ladies' man and a man's man—and a very successful man, to boot.

He was interested in marriage—at least in sociological and psychological facts about it—and quizzed her at their breakfasts. "Is living together before marriage a good way to reduce the chances of divorcing? Are children better off in stepfamilies than in single-parent families if the kids' parents are divorced?" And she'd shoot off the answers with glee—"Nope to the first, nope to the second"— as if they were playing an exciting parlor game. She ran a news show, after all.

Edward didn't chart her comings and goings, didn't want to chat too much at the end of the day, and had no apparent need to control Bess. He didn't find her energy and forthrightness daunting. He left to her all decisions about where to go and what to do when they were together, and she appreciated his willingness to let her lead the way. If she didn't handle things, though, they ended up with no real dates, just catch-up phone calls, six-word e-mails, hurried breakfasts. So she became assertive. "My place Tuesday?" she wrote in a decisive e-mail.

"Eggs and toast?"

"Thick steak, grilled. Eight p.m."

Like that. Once a week. Whatever she wanted, wherever she wanted. As long as it wasn't on a weekend.

The cloudy figure of a woman loomed in the background, someone whom Edward said he didn't live with and clearly didn't travel with and who didn't seem to mind what he did, but was just there, living somewhere in Texas. While he spoke (in his easygoing way) of imminently "letting her go," whatever her name was, months went by, and he never announced that he actually ended it.

Bess found out through someone on her show who knew Edward that this woman's name was Sally, but she was so in the background that Bess found herself dismissing Sally just the way Edward did. She moved increasingly into the role of the seductress, a role she'd never been in and that she kind of liked. Just as she'd become assertive about breakfast, she became assertive about sex— had to, or it might not happen. "Did I care whether he became free? Not really. I wasn't looking for forever; I wanted an affair. I *was* free, after all. "

And then, when sex did happen, it was as lovely as she'd imagined. Not fast and furious, as it had been with men for whom she'd had a mad attraction: This was slow, careful, dreamy sex.

She was oddly charmed, too, by his remarks, over two separate breakfasts, about loneliness in America. "Does this mean you're lonely?" she asked directly, as usual.

He answered her seriously, citing numbers he'd memorized: the 90 million single people in America, the 55,000 lonely people who log on to an Internet dating site every day, the $185 million they spend to find mates. He spoke about one matchmaker who said on *60 Minutes* that she earned upward of $5 million a year and got "marriage bonuses"—rings, cars—if her matches made it to the altar.

Bess took his meaning to be that he was *very* lonely.

Months later, when she asked Edward directly why, since he was clearly interested in her and ostensibly planning to get free of the relationship with this Sally person, he was so reticent about sex, so cautious, so *not* assertive, he explained that this was just the way he was. He believed in fidelity. Bess thought his rectitude charming and quaint, even though he clearly hadn't thought it through. They were, after all, having sex. He was, after all, still involved elsewhere. But on some level at least, he was uncomfortable sleeping with two women at once, or else he wanted her to think so. He also apparently wanted to wait until all signs were "Go" and spoke of "the winter" as the defining moment of the beginning of what he always referred to as their "partnership." Meanwhile, they continued doing what they were doing: occasional dinners, occasional sex.

Still smarting from the end of a relationship with another Drama King, Bess was happy to keep it light. She decided Edward's involvement with this mysterious Sally, whoever she was, served both of them. She wanted her autonomy, her full emotional freedom, and she liked their weekly liaisons. She didn't need aggression—straight-out or passive—from a man at this point in her life.

Months later, Edward was still reticent, still speaking longingly of "getting free" and still in no hurry. The roles felt reversed: She felt like the knight in a medieval courtship, hell-bound to get the lady to love him. She didn't mind the role reversal; she figured that when he was ready, he'd come on stronger. "When?" she once asked sweetly over poached egg whites at the hotel breakfast room they frequented on Thursday mornings.

"In the winter," he said with a smile. "I'm working it out with my therapist."

The EGG—the Easygoing Guy—so friendly, so attractive, so subtly, characterologically mysterious, is a magnet for strong, high-achieving women, particularly those who have recently tangled with invasive, critical, bullying Proprietors. He's the opposite of the bully: He's so absorbent, accepting, proud of a woman's strength and her achievements, and respectful of her autonomy. He's not jealous, not crazy, and willing to share her with her family and her work. He's someone who doesn't ask much, who seems pleased with the amount of attention he gets and unconcerned about whether the amount of attention he gives is enough. He likes strong women and depends on them: Edward asked Bess's advice about his speeches and his staff meetings and the annual reports, included her in his business problems, and sought her counsel about nursing homes for his mother.

But between dates, she was on her own. When they spoke on the phone or communicated by e-mail, Edward never concerned himself with whether the last conversation was hurried, or if Bess was under stress, or if there was any tension in her voice, or if she was off to the Coast. Those tiny signs of intimacy and despair lovers love to share were shared *when they were together*, but they didn't seem, somehow, to stick.

He's not insensitive, the EGG. He's just not terribly involved. He's not disinterested; his interest just doesn't go anywhere. It *seems* to—he occasionally refers to the future, unlike the Visitor—but it doesn't.

The EGG is not to be confused with the Visitor, despite their similarly casual ways. The Visitor comes and goes—physically. He shows up and doesn't show up. The EGG is there—but he's not *all* there. He's present, but not entirely, not all the way. He likes you, but he doesn't *get* you. They both manage presence and absence, but differently. The EGG, unlike the Visitor, can plan ahead. He doesn't seem afraid of involvement.

Women who've been with an EGG often bring up his past. They say he admits to having functioned for a long time inside a relationship that was either abusive or unhappy or in some way deeply troubled—but he doesn't seem to know what to make of that relationship. It's as if he knows it was terrible but also *doesn't* know, so he relates the traumatic little pieces of it—screaming battles, weeks without conversation—but is capable of delivering this information with a detached smile, as though he's waiting for someone to say, "That's just awful!"—but can't quite say it, know it, himself. At first, Edward seemed to be so delighted to be in this healthy dynamic with Bess, so surprised to be with a woman as savvy and accomplished as he, and so kind to him. He seemed hungry for something, but it wasn't clear what—as if he'd given up on the possibility of having the very "partnership" he spoke of so longingly, even as he was experiencing it.

"It was never clear to me whether he was wishing for more or vaguely in over his head," Bess mused, "because he was so simultaneously present but wistful and elusive. He said things like, 'I've always wanted this.' But the 'this' was murky, and I often wondered what it meant. It's not sexual. It's not intimate. It's promising . . . but it's not . . . there."

So Bess found herself saying things like, "I don't know what the 'this' is that you're referring to, but here we are. Let's have whatever it is you want."

Out of annoyance, she'd try to pin him down about small things. "You sounded busy when we spoke yesterday; what was going on?" and "Remember that contract I told you I was negotiating?" She was hungry for contact and continuity. "He doesn't remember the details," she said, with a little irony, "but is real glad my contract is going through. Not so glad that he wanted to celebrate, but pleased that I told him."

There is nothing lavish in this guy, no magnanimity. His attractiveness lies in his intelligence, his niceness, even a certain apparent docility, as if he's used to having to hand himself over to the relationship he's in. He's neither prickly nor skittish, neither stubborn nor willful. He's far more clearly attracted to strong women and not so obviously fearful as other Drama Kings are. He is nevertheless somewhat elusive. He's vague. Still, the fact that he showed up was enough for Bess, as it had been enough for other women—Sally, too, no doubt.

He told Bess he loved her energy; her "sunshine," he called it. (Strong women, take note: Drama Kings often see you as the sun. Nice, except that they then feel like smaller planets doomed to revolve around you.) Her extraordinary life force made him feel, he said, as if he might absorb some of her energy. The compliments he gave her always seemed to suggest an osmotic attachment—as if he deeply understood how dazzling she was and how crucial to his well-being. He seemed somewhat envious, as if he couldn't figure out how to have the light emanating from *him*, and maybe she would even teach him her trick; maybe if she could infuse him with some of that radiance, it would take hold in him and he'd generate his own—as though only then would he have something concrete to offer.

"I've always wanted a partnership, one that could be like this," he told her for the umpteenth time.

One time, she said, "Like what, Edward?"

"You're not like the others," he groped. "You're not as needy."

Bess jumped on it: "Not *needy?* Why would that be a good thing?"

He sighed and said he didn't really know. He looked tired.

Once they saw each other a little more regularly, and the "partnership" began to take hold, she instinctively began protecting him from the boring, dull, menial, and generally unpleasant tasks of daily living—he was just too busy and adorable to have to deal with all those little things that had to get done around the house. Charm, not involvement, was his strong suit (EGGs are often in the arts—they're the "talent," the artists, the actors, the singers, the writers, the "creative" people in companies). In exchange for having his life increasingly taken care of, for having intimacy readymade by a strong woman, Edward offered gratitude of a sort ("How is it you are so strong but also so womanly?") but revealed just the teeniest bit of chafing as well ("I'm not quite ready yet for our partnership; is that still okay?"). He spoke again of the winter, when things would work out between them, and of finishing therapy at the same time. "All my baggage is about to be deposited," he said mysteriously.

Bess didn't push it because, very simply, she was too busy. She wasn't sure she wanted much more of him, in terms of time, so she wasn't waiting for his verdict. What she wanted from him was more sex and less conflict about it; she so loved the easy, friendly, languorous way he had in bed. *That's* why she looked forward to winter.

Over the autumn months, Bess found herself becoming not Edward's mother, exactly, but something even more complicated— a support team: his manager and front man and shrink and best friend—all the can-do handlers who help get important people through life on time and unfettered by obligations and other irritants. She had them, too, the helpers, but she was used to them. He was not, and as a result of having them all in one—in her—he was becoming ever more sure of himself. She said:

It happened so gradually, I truly didn't realize the role I was cast in. In retrospect, I always was aiding Edward in some way— helping him in his business, with his accounts, mostly by e-mail.

As I slowly handed over the vertebrae of my backbone to Edward, he became straighter and stronger, but I obviously was losing little bits of what held me up. Like, disks. I didn't experience it that way, but I did become a little . . . wobbly. And my back hurt! Like, what was going on here? And you know, I'm not sure he didn't feel totally entitled to all of me, like it was his due—despite his reluctance to reciprocate, his deference, his guilt.

Winter came and went. She was traveling too much to ask him what was up. She was seeing other men desultorily and focusing on her darling baby girl, not so much a baby anymore at the age of eight, and working ungodly hours at the show. She just liked the EGG, that's all.

"I loved the sense of calm and quiet surrounding him," she said. "I loved his slow way of moving, of talking to me when we were making love. I still loved his sweetness—even if it was offered only when it was not needed."

Over time, though, as nothing much happened from one breakfast to the next, she began to feel vaguely used. But she didn't quite know what she was being used for—certainly not for sex. She began noticing, too, that on some level, she'd been trying to prove herself to him, to woo him, win him. She did this almost reflexively, not consciously. Consciously, the fact that he wasn't all that deeply "into" her didn't fully register; his elusiveness—a wistfulness, really—had become woven into their dynamic. Not accustomed to being incidental in someone's life, though, she thought that at any moment he'd wake up, drop his mysterious noncommittal façade, and declare himself mad for her.

What was he wistful about? Was it that hard getting free? Was Sally—the mystery woman whom he never seemed to be with or mention—giving him trouble? I didn't want to confront the fact that after almost a year of constant e-mails and Tuesday mornings and occasional evenings, he was still so essentially— sexually, emotionally—unavailable. Still so willing to keep things the way they were and yet so evidently sad about it. That he could still be fed, propped up by me. That he could keep promising in such a weird, vague way.

He was only adoring the Woman behind the Scenes, unobtrusive, never calling attention to herself, cheerful. I was acting the role of First Lady. Strong, quiet, undemanding, understanding, a rock. By casually playing handmaiden and superagent and confidante—which I do easily— I enabled him to continue looking as wonderful as the rest of the world had declared him to be. I had become a coconspirator! An enabler!

One rainy day in late February, Bess told Edward she was dating other men, which she figured he must have known, but added that she thought it best if they took a little break. Crestfallen, he agreed. "I guess I haven't figured out how to have what I want so very much," he said. How to have that oft-discussed partnership with her.

In other words, Sally was still there.

A t a dinner party with a crowd of television people in Los Angeles later in the month, Edward's name was mentioned. The guest who brought it up, Steven, worked with him as a copywriter at the West Coast branch of his agency. Steven was obviously unaware of Edward's involvement with Bess, and Bess didn't mention it.

Steven, hired four years earlier, spoke admiringly of the agency and of the team of mostly male account managers and copywriters that filled the three offices—Dallas, New York, and Los Angeles, He liked the mood there—said it was fun. The West Coast branch and the East Coast branch had a kind of hail-fellow rivalry, "an old-boys club," he said, while the Texas office was, well, "wild." They shared something else: a love of practical jokes.

After listing some of the better jokes they had played on one another—one elaborate joke had to do with an account manager who ended up flying to Cuba rather than to the Caribbean—Steven told of an agency-wide dating secret all the single men shared. "We all have a 'Sally,'" he said mischievously. He told three stories about these sought-after men, mostly in their twenties and thirties but many—"more than you would think," he said, in their forties and fifties—who had pretend girlfriends.

Bess was stricken: What was he saying? Her heart was pounding as she tried to figure out what this man really meant. Did Edward's Sally not exist? Was that *possible?* Could he really have played this tawdry, school-kid "joke" on *her?* Was "Sally" just a name, a shill, a device he used to protect himself—a sophisticated man of forty-five—from becoming available to her?

"Neat, eh?" Steven went on. "Sometimes even I believe my own Sally is out there somewhere."

The guests laughed uncomfortably, the way they do at stupid sex jokes.

"Wasn't there a movie about that?" one dinner guest asked disinterestedly.

Bess felt sick and excused herself.

"Yeah," she heard Steven's date muse as she made her way to the bathroom. "I forget the name of it, but it was with Cary Grant. Oh, wait . . . *Indiscreet*, I think."

One of her friends thought it was funny.

"What's funny about it?" Bess asked.

"I guess that you expect too much of men," the friend responded wearily, and for just one moment Bess was filled with an old sensation, one that she remembered from many years before. *Hey, Sweetheart, men are hard to figure*, her friend was saying, just as friends had said for the last thirty years. *But heck, all's fair, right? He's ambulatory and not gay, so he's a great catch! He's not crazy, right? He has a good job, no? So there's a little competition in the woman department. Go for it!*

Another friend said it was disgusting. "Remember that 'compliment' he offered up early on—the one about how you were not like other women because you weren't as needy? The man was trying to tell you something. It wasn't a compliment, it was a warning: Don't need me, Baby. I'm not available."

The flip side of this mild-mannered, unproblematic, dutiful fellow with the promise of a "partnership" just around the corner is that he refuses to make the "switch" he has expressed a desire to make. He evades emotional demands. Such a man will show up, no doubt, as Edward always did at Bess's, in the flesh but not in the spirit. He's longing for love, or seems to be—but he's somewhere else, spiritually, emotionally. He's unavailable.

And about that early compliment—the EGG has a fantasy woman in his head. In real life, he always offers congratulations for what he thinks a woman is *not*—"You're not a ball buster like other strong women," he'll say fondly. "You're not as demanding as other women in your field," or "You're not as aggressive as most high achievers I know." They put ambitious or aggressive or demanding or needy women into one category—and you, for the moment, in another. The fact that he's making invidious comparisons not with any real women but with old, hackneyed stereotypes—the clinging vine, the voracious sex demon, the killer city broad—goes by you. He speaks seriously about "types" of people. You know there's something troubling about his worldview, but it's not worth challenging his compliment with a grumpy, "Gee, sounds like you're not all that fond of strong women," or "That isn't really a compliment at all, now is it?" He won't answer because he doesn't really know.

But your instinct nailed it: His "complimenting" is a warning. The man who praises you in advance for *not* having certain qualities is a man who obviously doesn't want you to have them. The "compliment" is not about you, it's about him—and the fearsome traits he doesn't like. Does he criticize his ex-wife or ex-girlfriend for having these traits? Do you find yourself telling other people that his ex was "a real bitch"? Have you bought into his fears about women—and are you perpetuating them by trying to avoid being like those women? Are you busy forming yourself around a compliment that's really a putdown? Most of all, do you end up feeling either too needy, too demanding, too overwhelming, or too sexual? A real bitch? I'll bet you do.

Bess actually remembered the following conversation on their second breakfast "date." "You look so healthy!" he said. "Like someone who doesn't get sick a lot. I like that!" You bet he does. His response to any deficiency at all—like over-the-top anxiety or blind fatigue or even a long, bad cold—is as bland and passive as the rest of him, and even if you are privy to his Blackberry number, and even if you do break all your own promises and call him, he won't get back to you promptly. Remember how erratic his calls have been? How pleasant but withholding, and wistful, he seems when you're together? How he hands all the plans, all the sexual advances, all the *everything* over to you? How he cares so little about your emotional state? Now, when he's facing a demand for more attention or a plea for help or—horrors—a demand for more than his vague presence, his wrist will get numb, his hand paralyzed; his phone receiver will turn to lead, his hearing will fail—and his Blackberry will go on the fritz. He won't know why. He'll offer vague answers to your direct questions. He won't know what to do.

"Why do I feel as if I'm chasing you all the time?" asked Bess, direct as always, and finally getting tired of doing the chasing.

"I don't know. Maybe I haven't been as responsive as you'd like?"

"Yes, that's it! You haven't!"

"Yeah, maybe you're right."

And so it goes. He didn't deny it; he even confirmed it. He only denied . . . Bess.

Bess's mother died that same spring. Edward was so dutifully responsive but so formal, so polite, so clear about his peripheral involvement, that Bess was frankly stunned—a blow that intensified her grief. She remembered his warnings, framed as compliments, about how needy and sickly she was not. She realized, now that she was clearly as needy as he hoped she'd never be, how needed he refused to be. She'd betrayed him! Because of her mother's death, *she* was now the demanding Other, the needy wreck, the stereotype he set her up to be!

Yikes! She was now like his last girlfriend, or wife, or wives—or the "Sally" of these Drama Kings' nightmares. She's a woman, after all. And with any woman, deep down, the EGG feels he's being violated, called on to do something impossible—not just to be giving but something more challenging. The perceived demand makes him angry on the deepest level, and underneath the anger is the belief—and every EGG shares it—*that he doesn't have it to give.* He doesn't always know this consciously, of course, but all those earlier signs of inaction, inattentiveness, inertia—the promises of a future partnership "in the winter"—only testify to his decision not to be there. Bess remembered how, busy as she was, she always wound up feeling depleted, confused as to what was going on with Edward—with them. That was his hostility, and it was as powerful as if he'd whacked her on the head.

Not that he ever would. The EGG won't fight openly; when he doesn't want to play, he plays dead—he'll suddenly have to go tend to "Sally." Therein lies the distinction between him and the true passive aggressive. Alvin Blaustein, MD, a psychoanalyst in New York City, calls this type of man passive inadequate. He doesn't just torture you by the usual passive-aggressive means: being chronically late, forgetting to give you your phone messages, dropping your best china on the floor by mistake—often—or smiling when he delivers bad news. Instead, he "becomes disabled, emotionally and spiritually, at the moment you need him most. And he isn't able to pick himself up once he's down—he just gets more hopeless," says Dr. Blaustein. "He won't argue or confront; he'll just fade away and let you know by his actions that he isn't up to it—whether 'it' is marriage, fatherhood, a consistent career effort, whatever it is he doesn't feel up to. But of course, he never promised you anything, did he? His behavior just looked like it was moving in a promising direction. He can waste years of your life—and have you wind up feeling sorry for him."

Bess didn't feel sorry for Edward, fortunately. "I don't care why he needs to use a fake girlfriend. I don't care that he thinks he can't cut it or that he's terrified of being needed or that he's afraid of everything. I long since dropped the idea that I could make a baby-man, no, an embryo-man, grow up. I'm out."

Some Drama Kings can fool you: They don't embody drama, but they always *cause* it.

Telltale Signs of an EGG

1. He always has a laid-back, easygoing manner. This manner belies an intense and self-involved personality that is anything but low key or carefree. His typical greeting is a big, warm bear hug, accompanied by "Hey there, Gorgeous!" or "Oh, do you feel good!" He has a slow, lovely, lethargic feeling about him—and it takes a while to detect the cool, steely detachment that governs his life. His performance is a good one; he seems more *accessible* than other Drama Kings. Your impulse is to invite him over, tell him about a great show, push him into action. He is willing. "Sure, Babe! You just name it," he'll say.

At first.

Warmth and ease notwithstanding, he will nevertheless undoubtedly leave the actual pursuing to you. He may seem interested and available, but you'll find yourself angling to pin down that next meeting with him. You'll talk for hours, and then he'll happily leave with a "Hey, nice talking to you!" (or, more horrifyingly, "Have a great day!") exit. Easygoing is a pace as well as a style—and that pace is slow, which means he can wait longer than you can to hook up, hang out, or make an actual date. And that you will—now and forever—be the aggressor.

2. His life is very private and even mysterious. You quickly sense that you're not really a part of it. This is tricky, because he's available, sort of—he's just got many plans and schemes that don't include you. One woman who'd been with an EGG for two years said he bought a townhouse without so much as mentioning it to her until the deal was done and he was about to move in. "You have a new home?" she said, somewhat alarmed.

"Yep," he said.

"May I see it?" she asked.

"Sure, Gorgeous," he replied.

She wished she hadn't asked to see it but instead had simply never seen him again. Her EGG saw no reason to include her and no reason to explain why he just didn't. She was incidental to him.

3. Good sex always takes him by surprise. Because women are so incidental, he often seems taken aback when he's affected positively by one. "Boy, Babe, that was really good," he says, as if he'd forgotten that it was good the last time, too. Sex isn't what motivates him. Or rather, intimacy isn't. You always have the feeling that you're saying, "See? We have so much going for us," when in truth he's not all that interested. The trick is to believe that and accept it and not take it as a signal to try to make him more so. You can't.

4. Most EGGs have secret lives. The "Sallys" may be pretend or real. EGGs keep women on the side that they sleep with but don't love (you're one of them, by the way), and there are women they like a lot but don't sleep with (only you can say if this is you, too, later down the line). This is the way they like their lives set up—they're very organized creatures—and they're as cold-blooded as snakes about keeping it that way.

5. EGGs like to fantasize about relationships. Think of the way Edward fantasized about the "partnership" he so desired. But because EGGs feel inadequate and know on some deep level that they're not going to be able to have what they want, they feel defeated. That's the wistfulness you detect, the "if only" feeling they exude. EGGS yearn and they hope, but they know they're going to let themselves down. They can't reach out for what they really want, and they won't let anyone reach inside them. Unlike the Visitor, who doesn't want anything other than to visit, the EGG has this huge yearning for more, but also a profound and rather smug and complacent understanding that he won't get it.

Myths about the EGG

He's a sensitive guy, an artist; he's more like you than other, more testosterone-driven men. He wants to connect. I don't know about those men, but this one is tops at what is called highly skilled impression management. He's a Drama King, remember: a performer. All the tactics the EGG uses are part of a performance. But unlike skilled, professional actors, whose years of training teach them to reveal themselves to an audience, his particular brilliance is his ability to avoid detection in his grand scheme *to stay closed; not to connect!* The impression he gives is of the great communicator, the warm relater. It's an act. He's closed off; shut down.

Why You Were Taken In

You needed to enjoy, not fear, taking the lead in initiating sex.

You needed to feel free to discuss sex without immediately raising suspicions of sex with someone else.

You needed to reverse the equation I spoke about earlier, in the principle I call the Power of the Least Interested—that is, you needed, for one reason or another, to take the lead, to be *more* interested in connecting than he was. Perhaps you'd been with a smothering Proprietor. The EGG is the perfect respite from intensity and invasion—for a while.

The Easygoing Guy is the cozy image of a warm, affectionate guy. He looks the part and presents himself that way. He's sexy— or, more precisely, he's cuddly-*looking* and has an affectionate *manner.* Like a big, darling sheepdog or a golden retriever pup.

One woman said it took her a year to realize that just because her EGG would scoop her up in his arms each time they met and say, "Hey, Gorgeous!" that didn't mean what it seemed. It didn't mean he loved her. It's terribly confusing to be with a flattering man who is simultaneously closed off and detached.

His lovers soon find themselves on the lookout for his *negative* compliments, the "praise" he offers for being a woman "unlike all others." This awareness, they say, is transformative; it allows them to locate the source of their sense that they are, however obliquely, being put down in the middle of a "compliment." Discussing it rarely works: The EGG inevitably offers the disingenuous "Can't you take a compliment?"

But the growing awareness of the mechanism helps women feel less angry—and more knowing. What a transformation it is, from warding off hostility to facing it. This is one of the great strengths women receive, like unintended gifts, from Drama Kings, who so shamelessly chip away at women's pride. When Bess became aware of these negative compliments, for instance, she took charge of her part in the deal.

> It took me several months to know I was feeling dissed, deprived, and disappointed—not merely tired. It's hard enough to admit you have needs to a world-class nurturer, let alone someone who wants nothing to do with nurturing but pretends he does.
>
> The world gives wildly mixed signals about how best to meet the new, complicated requirements for women, and the last thing I needed was a man who gives me signals that add up to, "No, no, don't!"
>
> When I closed the door on all future breakfasts and steak dinners with Edward, I had the most amazing sensation. I didn't feel like a failure. I didn't feel as if I'd wasted time. I didn't wonder if, had I been cuter, thinner, bigger-breasted, sexier, I'd

have won him. I didn't have that sinking feeling of "What now?"
I simply felt great. Sprung. No regrets.

At the end, some women report an overwhelming sense of sadness, or frustration, because the promise of a real relationship was
so physical, so palpable. Most come to feel they have been duped.
At first, it felt counterintuitive, the idea that this adorable, manly
guy (one woman described him as that guy in all the ads at Christ-
mastime, the big cute one walking through the gentle snow with a
big red scarf around his neck, arriving at the door with piles of
Christmas presents in his arms) appears so promisingly protective
and turns out to be so irredeemably uncaring. The fantasy of
moving forward with this fellow, like the fantasy of moving to the
big city, quickly blows up once it's clear that what you hoped for
was affiliation, but what you got was alienation.

What You Learned from Him

The love lessons you learned with this careful, furtive, secretive
man were quite simple—but each one changed your perception of
yourself for the better. You learned to initiate sex. You learned to
be with a man who has a slow pace instead of a hurried one and not
to wrangle with it. You learned the distinction between approach-
able and *accessible*, between truly moral and sanctimonious. You
learned that sometimes an affectionate, affable demeanor is not in-
dicative of an expressive or easygoing inner life—that often, in fact,
it's a cover-up. Like microwaved meat, a man who is warm on the
outside can be icy, even frozen, on the inside.

Best of all, you learned to distinguish the difference between a
casual man in a warm relationship and a performer acting casual in
order to ward off relationship.

Bear in mind, just because you've been in a relationship with one Drama King, it doesn't mean you've developed immunity or even a second sense about another. As I said earlier, these men don't always reveal themselves immediately; they've got elaborate costumes and concealing scripts. But once you've been with an EGG (or a Visitor, a Proprietor, or any of the Drama Kings coming up), you're on your way to avoiding that type forever—and getting closer and closer to recognizing and honoring the importance of your own needs and desires.

Chapter Six

Drama King #4: The Hit-and-Run Lover

By you I was properly humbled. I came to you without a doubt of my reception. You showed me how insufficient were all my pretensions to please a woman worthy of being pleased.

—*Jane Austen*, Pride and Prejudice

On Kristin's thirty-ninth birthday, she got on a noon flight from Los Angeles. She had been back and forth between the coasts eight times since the beginning of the month in preparation for a dermatology conference, at which she was both chairing a committee and delivering a paper, and she was tired. At least she was in first class, or whatever it was that now passed for first class, she mused as she picked up the measly "bistro bag" outside the aircraft door—left there for coach passengers, but she took one anyway. She plopped down in the window seat in row two, buckled her seatbelt, and leafed through the airline magazine. She waited until the plane

119

took off and then turned on her notebook, put her earphones in, and began viewing the photographs of one patient's actinic keratoses, little "sun spots" she planned to remove soon as she returned home.

The man next to her in the aisle seat, wearing shiny, brown, tasseled loafers and tan corduroy pants in the middle of summer, kept looking down at her hands as she typed. He finally asked her where she was from, which was near his town in Connecticut, and what she did. Then he asked her outright, "I can't tell, with all those rings on your fingers. You married?"

"Oh, please," she thought, "not this."

"Yup," she lied.

Josh, the man most recently in her life, had come on to her in just this way about a year before—aggressively, with a barrage of personal questions, as if anything he wanted to know about her on their first meeting, however personal, she should confide immediately. This introduced her to a new kind of interaction: Unlike the fraught struggles she'd had before with an ambivalent Visitor, an invasive Proprietor, and an evasive Easygoing Guy, Josh had presented himself as eager—desperate, almost—to go out with her. *Out*—as in, to dinner, to the theater, to have fun. He had prodded her to date him just at the moment when she'd decided to focus on her practice and not be with another man.

"I want to see you," he'd said at the end of a dinner party at her friends Patricia and Howard's house near her hometown of Fairfield. She wanted to see him, too, and did for about a year. But then it became clear that her profession took too much time from the relationship and that despite Josh's stated desire for a high-achieving woman, in his heart of hearts he longed for someone—clearly not a doctor—who could pay more attention to him. The relationship ended.

The man next to her turned to her and said, "You're not really married, are you." Like that: A statement, not a question.

She felt herself getting defensive. The plane seats were annoyingly close to one another. She turned and looked him in the eye. "No, I'm not," she said, "but it's really none of your business, is it?" She smiled her most efficient brush-off-but-polite smile and, realizing she had said all this particularly snottily, added, "Sorry, but your question reminds me of a kid trying to hook up."

He considered this. "Hook up, eh? That's where you get together to have sex but it's all very casual? No, I don't do that." He said "casual" as though the word were new to him. His smooth, unlined face made him look to be in his late thirties, but his thick white hair, probably gray when he was in his twenties, suggested a little older. So did his bemused contemplation of the younger ways of coming together. "But I do date," he said brightly, as if she'd asked. "The old-fashioned way. I'm obviously not modern."

She looked at his old-fashioned loafers and said nothing. Neither was she, come to think of it. Modern.

"Will you have dinner with me Saturday night? A real date? The best Italian place in New Haven? I'll pick you up and take you home? The normal thing men and women do?" He took off his glasses and put them down on the tray table, as if to make better eye contact. His expression was sweetly beseeching. "Please?"

Unlike other men whose ambivalence blazed out from their chests like a P-Diddy diamond necklace even as they asked her out, there was no hesitation here.

"No? Then when? How about Friday? Saturday, then? Or a drive on Sunday to the shore—clams Casino at this amazing little spot, with fabulous Bloody Marys to wash them down? Did she like the theater? Chinese food? Bowling? Pub-crawling? Anything?"

She was oddly charmed—How do these guys *get* this kind of aggression? Testosterone alone? Do they take assertiveness training in the womb?—and a little taken aback. "Why are you in such a hurry?" she asked.

"No time," he said evenly. Her fear of too-much, too-soon seemed so dull and self-protective, suddenly, next to his vividly articulated vision of great meals and togetherness and willingness to go play—a good time, he insisted, just awaiting her okay.

"The thing is, I'm still otherwise engaged," she announced. He didn't have to know she wasn't. He didn't have to be informed that as of late, she had developed an aversion to relationships. "Sorry. Really, I am."

He backed off in time for the in-flight movie, and she thought that was that.

Afterward, though, just as passengers were pulling the shades up, revealing a cloud formation she recognized as a "mackerel sky" that indicated rain, he chatted her up again, but this time without mentioning their getting together. His name was Greg, and he was an art dealer. Freelance, based in New York City's Soho district. Married for six years and divorced last January. Joint custody of one child, a three-year-old boy named Joey, and a decent relationship with the ex-wife, but fear that she was going to move away with the child or not let him see him.

She got through the rest of the trip like that. Lots of talk. No more approaches.

So when he called her at her office at eight the next morning, she didn't know how he'd gotten her number. She was rattled. "How'd you find me? she asked.

"You're a doctor. You're listed," he said. "I just called a little early, is all. But I thought I'd leave a message. I'm thinking, though," he continued, "that instead of the Italian place, I thought we'd go into New York. To the best French place in the city. *Alain Ducasse.* Have you been?"

No. But Kristin felt more weary than charmed; it was too soon for this kind of persistence, and she thought she'd made her position clear the night before—how much clearer could "buzz off" be? She didn't feel like being flirtatious, coy, or adorably game; this whole business just made her tired.

"Thank you, but no. No, I haven't been, and no, I don't want to go. Look, the truth is, I'm a complete workaholic. Trust me."

A long pause. "Okay, Doc," he said. "But I'm not going to give up." There was another pause. "Shall I read the pause as an opening?"

She hung up.

The next day at noon, she received a call from the receptionist at the office she shared with four other doctors. "Lunch is here," Jeannie said. "Compliments of a 'Greg.'"

Kristin opened a large package from a sushi place near Yale University, where her office was. In it was an elaborate display of sushi and sashimi in a black lacquer dish; a side order of marinated spinach called *oshitashi*, her favorite; and green tea in a thermal cup. (Where did *that* come from? she wondered.) Finally, pineapple, lychee, and a jellylike confection covered with powdered sugar. The note said, "So, how about Japanese?"

She was hungry, so she ate it. And she did have to thank him, but he brilliantly had included no phone number. "You're welcome," he said when he called late that afternoon. She didn't pick up. The words were scrawled on a pink "Who Called" note left on Kristin's desk by Jeannie before she went home.

The lunches kept coming. No more notes, no phone calls, just delicious, glorious lunches from the best places in town. Seems Greg and Jeannie were in cahoots—he'd call each morning and ask if Kristin had a lunch date, and if she did, he wouldn't send lunch; otherwise, along it came. Jeannie loved him. Everyone who heard about him loved him.

"Thank you," she said at the end of a week, when he called. "But please, I'm getting fat. No more." She didn't want to think about any other possible analyses of his behavior—buying her affection, passive aggression ("You want to say no to *me?* Good luck."), hostility of the bullying sort.

Is this how sexual harassment begins—so pleasing, so innocuous? It wasn't clear to her whether she should refuse to receive the meals, and she didn't want to spend the time finding out how to reach him in order to discourage him. She figured it would peter out soon enough. The truth was, though, she half welcomed the lunches and was somewhat titillated by this odd magnanimity and display of interest. On the other hand, what kind of doctor, or woman, accepts lunch every day from a stranger?

"I figure if you get fat enough, you'll have no one to date but me," he told her at the end of the second week, at which point she had begun taking his calls. "Speaking of which, wanna try dinner instead of lunch?"

"Please," she said quietly, in her nicest voice. "I've told you before, I'm just too busy. So no more sushi. I appreciate your . . . kindness," by which she meant his tenacity, "but please, no more food."

"I'll wait," he said.

Her heart started beating in rage. How could he be so undaunted? What would do it? *"Fuck off?"*

The lunches stopped and the phone calls dwindled, finally. She was getting her act together, she told herself. She was learning to live, really live, without a man—not just bide her time. She'd altered her expectations profoundly since the end of her affair with Josh. With her work taking up the weekdays and nights, her life was just the way she wanted it, even if it wasn't what her mother had had in mind for her. As she told me:

> *I was content. I wasn't waiting for anything to happen, particularly not with a man. I didn't need anyone to save me, help me, do for me, or be anything to me. The idea of a man coming*

*into my life and throwing me back to where I used to be—where
I always was with a man—had finally, finally lost all its appeal.
I'm not saying that was final, or forever, but definitely for now.*

Then she saw Greg again. In a restaurant called Sakura in
Westport, forty-five minutes south of New Haven. She'd been
seated in the back, in the "traditional" Japanese dining area, with
her friend Ellie, and as they left the restaurant, Greg was leaving
the front grill area, where the chefs with their rapidly clicking
knives and the sizzling shrimp and steaks were. He saw her first. He
was with two other men.

"How was the sushi?" he said coyly as he introduced her to his
friends. And suddenly, just like that, Kristin decided she wanted to
see him.

"How about the new Thai place in Norwalk?" he whispered as
he was leaving. What guts; as if she'd never turned him down.

"Okay."

His almost imperceptible double take, nothing dramatic—as
though he didn't want to miss a beat—made her choke back a
laugh. She knew he was completely surprised. "Eight o'clock Saturday," he said coolly.

She smiled her assent.

And thus it began. Said Kristin:

> *I just got tired of my own defenses. They were so . . . trans-
> parent to me. Like women who've been burned by one guy and
> then forever after hold all men responsible. Anyway, Greg was so
> funny and dry and fabulous. He took me on with such complete
> ease and readiness. We became lovers that same night.*

He spoke of his dreams of family and homes with white picket
fences. He spoke of puppies and walks on the beach and introducing

her to his son and having more children. Kristin didn't want children, and the picture he painted was somewhat laughable to her—"like some tired old line used to appeal to women in those personal ads, with Walks on the Beach cited as the guy's favorite thing to do." But she was amused by the fact that *he* was the one taken by the fantasy and that he knew *she* wasn't interested in picket fences, puppies, and babies.

> *He had all these corny fantasies of a certain kind of love, ideas that haven't been around in decades. A small clapboard house. A station wagon—a woodie—not an SUV. I mean, where can you even get a station wagon anymore, let alone an item so out of date I think the Beach Boys used to sing about it? He wanted checks with our names on them, a joint account. A fireplace, a dog—named Spot! And he wanted it all* now. *He was passionate about the environment and world peace and. . . .*
>
> *He sounded like Miss America. I loved the whole business of being the cynic who was being dragged into this whirlwind of old-fashioned love. I started to think of wearing little 1950s hats—zillion-dollar retro frocks. And penny loafers, with socks. Tweeds. Jodhpurs. He'd have loved it.*

Then she was on a plane again, close to a year later, without Greg next to her, and she felt lonely for him and his perfect tasseled loafers and his endless easy chatter. They had spent a heavenly vacation in Aspen, where they were considering the prospect of buying a small condominium "down valley"—a gorgeous little place that was wildly expensive. They'd put in a low bid—too low, probably, they thought. But they were starting a life together.

When Kristin returned from her trip, she felt an odd tingling in her hands, a sensation that went all the way up to her neck. She also had a fever, which lasted a day and then went away. Had she been bitten by a tick? the doctor asked. She didn't think so, but she had walked in the woods in the conservancy a few times before she left. Then the fever came back a few days later. Her hands still tingled, and her knee and hip joints ached, and she had what must have been a migraine. She went back to the doctor for a blood test. Three days later, the diagnosis was clear: She had Lyme disease. She would have to go on antibiotics fast, but it was already too late to guarantee ridding herself of some of the symptoms. "The Lyme presents itself in many different ways," she was told. *The Lyme?* She might or might not have carpal tunnel, too, another possible explanation for the tingling in her hands.

She told all this to Greg, who departed from his usual total concentration and superhuman absorbency by looking stricken. "How sweet," she thought. "He's worried." He left her apartment, where he'd spent the night, saying he'd be back later or he'd call. She was gobbling antibiotics and giving orders to Jeannie on the phone about what to tell her patients as he got his things together and stopped for a moment beside her. She looked up to give him a kiss and saw he was agitated. He said, "I hope I can be there for you while you're so sick."

"Be there for you" raced through her head as a peculiarly modern construction for Greg, but all she said was, "You can, Baby. Just bring some aspirin when you come back, okay?" and returned to talking to Jeannie.

Greg didn't bring aspirin—because he didn't come back. Not that day or the next. Nor did he call.

At first—that is, later the same day—she simply called his cell phone. "Greg, you okay?"

He never called back.

Frightened, she left another message late that night. "Greg, this is scary. Let me know you're okay."

And then another, the next day. "Look, I don't know what's

going on. Take all the space you need—just please let me know you're not in trouble, or hurt. Leave a message on my cell phone. I won't pick up."

Nothing.

When three days passed, and she couldn't reach him by phone, e-mail, or through friends—who also hadn't heard from him, or so they said—and he hadn't responded to her pleas, Kristin became hysterical. Was he lying somewhere under a truck? Had there been some desperate family emergency? This was not like him. Sure, he'd gotten busy before. Sometimes didn't call right back. Sometimes went into funks when his ex-wife yelled at him or took his son on the weekends he was supposed to be with Greg. She tried once more: "Are you dead? You'd better be. This is sheer cruelty."

She called me when he didn't call her.

"I know it's weird that I waited this long to call you, but you know, he's got so much going on that I thought I'd hear from him within a few days. But it's been five days. And all I think about is, well, his ex-wife's pissed off all the time, and his son hasn't met me yet, and, well, he's got a lot on his mind. *Why the fuck am I making excuses for him?* What flaw in my character thinks there's some rational explanation for all this?"

She wanted to know, was he a multiple personality?

I t's the one situation a woman is never prepared for. A man who seems to have invented the words *passion* and *commitment* sails in, demands reciprocity, gets it—and then splits the scene. This darling, seemingly involved, sensitive Drama King turns out to be not what he says he is, not interested in what he says he's interested in, not someone who wants what he claims he wants. He's someone who cringes from reality behind the words he bandies about. He is a relationship creator but has no intention of having the relationship he creates. He only wants to woo you, not win you permanently. It's fantasy that charms him and both reality and relationships that depress him.

But he is shrewd. He isn't a multiple personality, a split personality, or even what shrinks would call a schizoid personality. He's the Hit-and-Run Lover.

Kristin thought of calling the police, the missing persons bureau, the emergency room. But then, at midnight, ten days after he disappeared, she finally got him on the phone at his apartment. "*You're not dead!*" she shrieked. "Thank God!" and blurted out something along the lines of was he okay. "I can't talk now," he said icily. "I'll be in touch."

Be in touch? Kristin, stricken, started poring over every moment of their last few times together, reexamining their words and the flavor of their interaction and their sexual connection and her behavior—over and over, she rehashed the minutiae of their last night together until, sicker than she already was, she threw up. "Is it because I got sick? Is it that we were about to buy property together? What? What?" she wondered. "What did I say?" She hated this line of self-inquiry, since she knew she hadn't done anything wrong. Yet here was her committed boyfriend of over a year—a man with whom she had bought a car and was about to buy a condominium in Colorado; a man who had proclaimed over and over that she was the woman of his dreams; a man whose parents she had met and loved—heading for the hills as if they'd had an unspeakable fight. Was he a serial killer? An axe murderer?

I follow stories of the Hit-and-Run Lover with weird fascination, knowing that even the more pathological ones are just one small step sicker than Greg. In June 1983, for example, Robert Maharam walked out of his Long Island, New York, home forever, leaving two typewritten notes, one to his wife of thirty-one years, Jane, and one to his grown daughter, Patsy. He not only walked out, he took everything in the house he could get his hands on: jewelry, art, all the cash kept hidden in secret places. He cleaned out their bank accounts; canceled the credit cards; and had secretly arranged to sell his share of the family business, which he had built over the years with Jane, and keep the profits. When a judge ordered him to pay Jane more than $4 million, he disappeared. Since then, he has never shown up, never paid. There's ample evidence of his existence and of his expenditure of their money—cruises and hotels all over the world have records of it—but no one can catch him. In an article in *New York* magazine, his daughter said, "He sat there and said, 'I've hidden all the money, and your mother's never going to get any of it.'"

The hit-and-run Drama King is always in love with a fantasy—whether of a perfect woman, a perfect life, or perfect financial bounty. He has to leave real life, since anxiety and resentment over it foster such an intense emotional aversion to the real people in it and the real troubles that he faces. He is, like every other Drama King, woefully inadequate to the task of having an intimate partnership, and he is therefore monstrously disappointing. Wooing allows him to appear able to commit, but more time spent in a relationship might bring deeper involvement, which would reveal him as the terrified, cringing creature he is. He's gone long before that can happen.

The variations are endless, the upshot incredibly familiar.

In a mere three months, Abigail reported to me, she'd designed and completed the most elaborate decorating job of her life. The fact that it was her lover's weekend home in Vancouver added to the challenge of turning in a magazine-quality renovation so quickly. The fact that the two were set to move into it together made it all the more fun to hurry it up. She thought it was her best work to date: coolly masculine enough for Hugh, who'd stipulated "no frilly stuff," and yet not too stark. She'd used texture—her trademark—for warmth. The rich damasks and heavy linens and cut velvets, all in shades of teal blue, seemed to open up the sky indoors; the project would only add to her reputation as the chicest decorator in Boston.

He'd pursued her. Begged her to fly up to this place in his plane to take a look at the property, then pressed her to be his lover. "When can I see you?" was a daily morning call. He wouldn't stop calling. Her "I don't go out with clients" reply was a pallid rebuff, since he wasn't yet her client when she said it. He simply pushed until she gave in. And then she fell in love with him, just as he'd hoped she would. She was as pleased with this relationship as she'd been with any intimate relationship in her life.

She adored his take-charge style—a style very much like her own. She adored, if the truth be known, being pursued. And when he arranged everything to Abigail's liking, even insisted the project be put on her own credit cards (with his bank automatically paying her back at the end of the month) so she could reap the mileage benefits, she declared this darling man of hers the perfect client, too. Then came gifts of gratitude for working so hard. Then plans for their future together in that knockout home.

Throughout the project, considerate client that he was, he refused to inspect the job. He occasionally looked distractedly at swatches, but his mantra was, "I trust you. I don't want to be in the way. I love teal blue.

"Go to it," he'd say.

The last month's bill was astronomical. Her mileage was, too. She'd be able to travel free and first class forever now, probably. How nice that Hugh's "Don't worry about the money" was coming from someone who *wasn't* worried about the money.

When Hugh finally walked through the finished house, the first thing she noticed was his uncharacteristic mumbling. "The tiles have a weird feeling underfoot," he said under his breath. "Why did you use that color for the couch?"

Omigod, this can't be happening, she thought as she heard herself say, "You said you liked the color."

"I'm going to have to do it all over," he mumbled finally, not looking at her. "It's all wrong."

As Abigail's story unfolded, right in the middle of it, I thought, I know this man. I know what he's going to do. I know him because I've heard about him so often over the past twenty years. I know it has nothing to do with the decorating job.

Abigail gathered her strength, there in their teal blue living room, and summoned the courage to question him, this man she loved so much, so they could figure out how to begin to fix what he felt was wrong. She was having an anxiety attack: What about *them?*

Why was he being so chilly, so implacable, so distant? How could she fix *that?*

He walked out, saying nothing, in the middle of her heart palpitations.

This darling, committed, loving man never spoke to her again. He changed the locks. Canceled the automatic payment to her at his bank. Changed his phone numbers. Gone. Another hit and run.

Abigail spoke to a lawyer months later about recovering the money Hugh owed her for the final bill—more than $65,000, spread out over two of her cards (one for American Airlines and one for Delta). The lawyer put it to her coldly: "And why again did you use your own credit cards?"

This is the kind of thing that used to happen to women but absolutely cannot happen to a strong, sophisticated, self-sufficient, powerful, successful woman like Abigail. But of course it does—to her and to all of us.

As Kristin struggled to understand the disaster that had just befallen her, she determined—idiotically, she said—that Greg left "not because I had told him I loved him—for hadn't he loved me, too?—but because just this once, in all the time we were together, I *needed* him."

Kristin was probably correct. Being counted on is just what the Hit-and-Run Lover resents most.

"I hope I can be there for you," he'd said. She mimicked the words. "What does that *mean?*" she asked for the thousandth time, first to Jeannie and then to me.

"It depends on how he defines 'can,'" Jeannie had replied miserably.

"Doesn't a person have to be in a *coma* not to respond? Not to show up for a lover or anyone else who's sick? I mean, I might wonder, if I were he, if I had the stuff to 'be there' for someone who was *dying* some godawful, gruesome death, but you can be damn sure I'd acquire it somehow if it didn't come naturally," Kristin said.

"He's a miserable man," Jeannie had agreed.

"Oh, please. He's a walking *mental illness*. But why didn't I notice? What were the signs? He was in love with me! He said so! He showed so! What set him off? What did I do? Could I have seen it coming? Jesus God almighty, I didn't have a clue! I mean *that* is what's *really* male here! He kept his inner life a complete secret and his outer self didn't betray it! Here's a relationship that's getting better and better, more ostensibly intimate, but the moment we face one of life's roadblocks—its smaller ones, I might add—he's out. How do I process the fact that he disappeared right in the middle of a *good* affair? A *happy* sex life?"

The stories of Hit-and-Run Lovers seem endless. Sandra, a well-known international opera singer, met Otto, a pianist and accompanist, in Vienna, where she was performing. He followed her back to San Francisco, where she lived. They were mad for each other. He was the lonely and talented child of Czech parents who got him out of the country when he was ten and sent him to music school in Paris; she was the lonely and talented child of African American parents who got her into Juilliard when she was in her teens. He married a French woman who, he said, left him five years before he met Sandra; she had never married. They were both thirty-five.

Sandra recalled:

We had just gone to a Christmas Eve party, a beautiful party in New York with a piano player from the City Opera of New York. I remember sitting around singing Christmas carols and drinking fabulous champagne and being so in love, and Otto being so happy. We had planned this trip to go out West mountain climbing—can you imagine, me, mountain climbing? But he had talked about it and talked about it, and so I said "Let's do it." I'd paid for our tickets, and we couldn't wait.

So here we were, glowing in that Christmas spirit, this sweet, sensitive, artistic man and me. We'd just spent a week up north at a farmhouse in Old Chatham and had come back for this Christmas Eve party. That night, we went to a hotel and made love, and when he got up to go back to his place, he looked at me with that wonderful, expressive face and said very deliberately, not offhandedly, "Sandra"—he pronounced my name Sawndruh— "I adore you. I just adore you." And I knew that he did. And he walked out, and I walked out, and then . . . I didn't hear from him.

Not at Christmas, not at New Year's. No "Merry Christmas," no "I was kidding about adoring you," no "Oh, by the way, I'm really not divorced from my wife," no nothing. Nothing. *I couldn't reach him on any phone. No one we both knew knew where he was. And I got the flu, needless to say, and was sick as a dog, had to cancel two performances, and he finally called right before our trip was to have taken place—it was coming up in about two weeks—and said, in this strained, terrible voice with that accent, "Sawndruh, I just cahn't do it."*

I said, not knowing what the hell he was talking about, "Can't do what?"

Can't do anything, as it turned out. He explained to me that his wife, the one who had left him five years before and had not been in contact with him since, had called him from Ukraine and said she wanted to "reconsider" their relationship, or maybe it was reevaluate it. I said, "What relationship? The woman left without a trace a thousand years ago. You're divorced." Really. I meant it; what relationship could there be with a woman who walked off with a rival pianist and went to live with him in God-knows-what country and sent him the divorce papers without discussing a divorce?

"Well, then, fine," I said, after wondering whether he really even was divorced. "Reconsider, then. But please pay for your ticket, since it was on my charge card. Mail it to me." And I hung up.

And he came over two days later—I was still sick, of course—and he said again, "Sawndruh, I just can't do it." And I said, "Get out of my house before I murder you. Just give me the money. And go." And I remember walking to the door, not in one of my gorgeous peignoirs that divas are supposed to wear, but in tattered flannel pajamas, no makeup, drooling and sneezing, and he said, "I'm so worried about you. I hope you feel better." And I just let out a scream. Not a high note. Not controlled. A scream that could have given me nodules on my vocal cords and ruined my voice. I slammed the door in his face.

I hope you feel better? *"Are you crazy?" I said. And he was so shocked at my response; so shocked that I screamed—singers don't do that. It was like something out of a Bergman film.*

I saw him in May at Lincoln Center. He came backstage. I nearly had a heart attack, looking at that skinny man and his haunted face and his pleading, guilty, miserable eyes. And he wanted to start up the relationship again! I have no idea whether he did or did not get back with his wife. But the idea of that man—can you imagine?—standing there, with that face, saying "Sawndruh, I just adore you." and then never calling again? It's as disturbed as it gets.

When I speak of relational strength, I mean the ability to be inside a relationship; that is, to bring one's authentic self into it and to be compassionate to one's partner. Both take certain skills, and it takes effort to develop those skills. Like any other art, intimacy takes time and interest and focus. The Hit-and-Run Lover doesn't want to develop this multifaceted kind of strength, or feels he can't. He can't say "no." He can't say, "That feels like too much to me." He just acts "yes" and finally does the "no" he couldn't say.

He feels he doesn't possess the tools or, possibly, the *authentic self*, to be truthful—and that reality leaves him with the knowledge that he's a fraud. Sandra said:

He once said to me, "If you knew how deeply depressed I can get, how deep I can go down, you wouldn't recognize me," and in fact, when I spoke to him once again, that's where he sounded. Like, in a hole somewhere in hell. It was almost too much for him, the sunniness of our relationship and my life and me—it's as if he was so essentially gloomy, and he was seeing some light, but it was blinding him. And it was too much for him to keep up that act, impossible to sustain that persona.

And by the way, he lied to me. He'd said he was divorced and in fact did get separated while he was with me. I think. Obviously, though, he went back. He operated so utterly believably. I mean,

I'm a sophisticated person; I understand acting and actors. I can see through falseness. Really. I'm trained in drama.

And then I remembered that he'd had another relationship during the time he was married, with a woman he also left and whom he then ran into years later. She apparently said to him, "Remember, I'm always available." I remember thinking, "Fool. I wouldn't be!" So this was a habit. It must have been a habit. He must wander around like this until his wife steps in like a watchdog.

There's only one thing to do when this creature has devastated and humiliated you: Pretend he never happened.

Tell yourself you were the victim of a natural disaster—a flood, a tornado. By no means indulge in an endless rehash of his behavior—"Which signals did I miss?" "What could I have said better?"—because it grants him a modicum of normalcy. No self-recriminations, either: Blaming yourself for the Hit-and-Run Lover is like blaming yourself for a hurricane.

Kristin couldn't have seen this coming. Not the first time, anyway. But in the future, there will be slight giveaways—tiny indications that a Drama King of the hit-and-run variety is on the prowl. His dream of the perfect little couple in the perfect little cottage—the pretense of normalcy implicit in that fantasy and the *uber*-prosaic quality of the lifestyle—and his assumption that you, as a woman, want the same thing, are part of the courtship plan and very shrewd, for even though Kristin did *not* want that darling little picket-fence scenario, she thought it charming that Greg did.

The Hit-and-Run Lover knows how bored women are with

men who won't commit, and he refuses to be boring. So he pretends. He wants so desperately to seem normal, when on some level he knows that he's not. He knows he hasn't the strength for an ongoing and committed relationship, so he fakes it. Hence the nonsense about the sweet little cottages and darling little puppies and all those clichéd signals of domestic bliss that he waves in front of you.

Also telling is the going-in-for-the-kill quality he has when he is after you. It seems flattering, but it's inappropriate. It feels like a need to have you that isn't *about* you.

And finally, the other advances, such as sending Kristin lunches against her will. She'd have had to send them back to stop them—like magazines she didn't subscribe to and didn't want. The Hit-and-Run Lover's desire to seem like the perfect catch is one of the saddest of all ruses used by Drama Kings, a way to bait you before switching into a hopeless disappointment. Because deep down he knows how unready he is, he's selling himself. And why didn't he want to know more about *you* instead of pushing to let you know about how he was Mr. Perfect? He wanted to chase you, not win you. He's just a run-of-the-mill commitment-phobe dressed up as some retro fantasy of the perfect husband-to-be.

It's instructive here to take a look at the Hit-and-Run Lover from his own point of view. I had one in my office not long ago, a man named Leonard, quite infamous among high-profile women for his sudden, inexplicable, devastating departures. He contacted me on another emotional matter, and he agreed to talk about his past. Leonard left a jazz singer after the two of them had bought a yacht together; just vanished somewhere into the Aegean. He agreed to speak to me about what goes on inside him when he bolts.

And boy, does he ever bolt! He's abandoned his last three lovers with the same impulsivity as Greg, with no warning, no advance weirdness, nothing a woman could look at in retrospect and say,

"Aha! There! That's when I should have known something was up!" The last departure was when Leonard had a date for Valentine's Day with a woman he loved and for whom he'd bought a lovely charm bracelet—with an engraved heart as the charm—from her favorite antique shop in Dallas.

But he never made it to dinner. And he never called to tell her he wasn't coming.

"So she was there, waiting for you, all dressed for dinner?" I asked.

"Yes," he said, looking me straight in the eye. Like, "You wanna know the truth? This is the truth. This is what I do, like it or not." He said:

> You never think, she may need me, or she may be desperate, or she may be in pain. The woman is the last thing on my mind. "I'm getting outta here"—that's what you think when you don't go pick her up. And "I got outta there" is what you think when you've left her flat. It's utter, complete relief, like you narrowly escaped a bomb put in your glove compartment.
>
> Later, the whole adrenaline thing goes away, and you're left feeling like a worm, a creature crawling around in a black hole you can't get out of. I eat when I'm there. Pizzas, Twinkies, Cokes. It's like kleptomaniacs: They get this amazing rush when they steal something, a sense of total victory, incalculable gain, but that feeling is all fueled by anxiety and need and desire and all those wonderful chemicals that flood you when you're high as a kite on your own brain juices. And then, bam! the kleptos get home with whatever they took and it looks nice and it's free and they won, but they go down, down as they realize it's all just as unsatisfying as the rest of what they own. It's similar: I go down, I crash, I realize my escape was all just part of a hideous cycle of sickness, and I can't move.

"Is it an act? That is, is it all a conscious plan—to win her and then drop her?" I asked.

"No. It's not an act," he said, "although I've repeated it often enough so you'd think I'd be hip to my own tricks. But I think, when I really like her, 'This time I'll follow through.' It's only when this thing goes off in my head, this alarm, this 'Oh, shit, I can't do this,' that I remember I've heard the same alarm, then done the same thing in response, many times before. So if it's an act, it's an unconscious one."

"Can you work?"

"Yeah. You can separate yourself into compartments. Work is okay. But at home I go back into the hole, with a new cocktail of chemicals. I become scared. I get consumed by the fear that if I telephone or stop by, she'll hit me with an avalanche of anger, so I never, ever do."

"But her anger never scared you before you bolted?"

"It's not about her anger, really, so no, she never scared me. It's not about her. It's so old, it's like the most primitive response, the most desperate 'Mommy's mad' kind of anxiety. And all you want is to avoid it; avoid her, avoid the rage."

"Do you ever have the sense that it's your own anger that terrifies you?"

"Yeah, sometimes, but that's too deep for what I feel. I just put it onto her, all the rage."

"Do you have any urge to speak to her? I mean, is there a desire to explain, or is there really nothing to say?"

"There's nothing to say. What excuse is there? And even months later, when you feel no more fear and sort of have this weird hankering to start up again, you remember what you've done. You don't really think you can say, 'Hi, there, remember me? The sick, cowardly one? I went underground for a while because I felt like I was going to die if we continued on together!' "

"Do you *think* about getting back together?"

"Not really. You know you've pulled the plug; that it's all over. You know you can't cut it, and you know *she* knows you can't cut it, and you know you're going to do it again, even if she doesn't know you will. And sometimes she doesn't; she thinks you've learned your lesson, and then you hate her for trusting you and think she's a moron if for some reason she talks about giving you another chance."

Leonard said he used to check out as abruptly as Greg did even if there was no crisis to prompt it. No sickness, no overt neediness on her part was the trigger. All it took was the merest perception that he couldn't fulfill his lover's expectations, whatever they were and no matter how minimal. Reconstructing his emotions before he bolts, he said:

> *I'm expected to be somewhere, do something, behave in a certain way. I know I won't be able to do it, so before I get found out, I check out.*
>
> *I can want to do it with all my heart, but what I know in that heart is that I won't be there. I just won't be there when she wants me, so I might as well make my departure an early one—not, say, on the plane headed for our vacation or at her aunt's funeral. I have the decency* [he laughs] *to make my exit the moment I know I'm not going to be able to do any more in the relationship.*

Clearly, this is the Drama King of all Drama Kings. There is none other in the pantheon who boasts this degree of separation from true connection, none who severs himself so dramatically, so totally, from contact. His is the performance, the acting job, of a lifetime: a man who is totally made up, from his purported dreams and aspirations to his ostensible desire for a strong woman. Aristotle said that character is revealed through action. By that definition, this Drama King's character, like that of a mole, is buried so far underground that any action aboveground is stifled—overwhelmed by air and light.

Interestingly, Leonard was famous for grand acts of attention—the sushi trays sent to the office were exactly the kind of thing he'd do, too; the darling T-shirts collected for his girlfriend from different places; the artwork and flowers and lovely scarves and designer sunglasses—all presented carefully, lovingly, with in-joke cards and beautifully inscribed notes. The notes would have special seals on the envelopes, "like from Romeo to Juliet," Leonard said. But these are shows of affection, of whimsy, and worlds away from feats of commitment. They always appeared out of the blue, on *his* terms, and were delivered, significantly, most often *before* the relationship got started, when he was still in seduction mode—the only mode, incidentally, that assuages the Hit-and-Run Lover's anxiety enough to free his generous impulses.

When the relationship happens, and the expectations begin:

I start to get that feeling, it's almost like nausea. It's truly disease. It's usually when the relationship starts getting warmer, and the woman mentions something to me that would ordinarily clinch the intimacy we'd built up together. Like suggesting a getaway over the winter or looking at dining room chairs for her place—which she maybe hopes is going to become our *place—anything that suggests we'll be seeing a lot more of each other in the future. See, for me it was all about wooing and winning, I guess. 'Cause the moment* she turns around and says, "You're *on! I love you! Let's go to Barbados!" I think, "Oh, God, I don't know if I'll be seeing her in the winter!" And I get panicky, and I have to go.*

It gets worse. He doesn't hear command voices in his head, which would suggest a legitimate psychiatric illness and a reason for all this—schizophrenia, say. No, he isn't compelled by voices, just compelled by instinct. Fight or flight. And at the same time that he cannot meet any needs, he also cannot tolerate any guilt feelings, so he has ingenious ways of blaming his behavior on his girlfriend!

"You don't just decide to exit and then exit," he says. "You feel it coming on, a growing discomfort between you that feels like the beginning of an infection. You feel it deep in your tissues some-where and then, *bam!* there it is. Like the flu."

Leonard finally learned in therapy to recognize his own symp-toms and to talk about them, not to act out in anger. "When the 'flu' hit, I used to decide she *deserved* to be deserted for not paying attention to my 'I'm about to desert you' signals—of which there were none. That's how nuts I was. I used to build up a dislike for her—she doesn't understand opera; my daughter may not like her; she wears funny clothes; she's too fancy, too smart, too rich, too strong, whatever—to convince myself that this wasn't going to work and that I'd better get out quick."

Oh, dear. An addict. A *bolting* addict.

Leonard now says he's had enough therapy to see an "emotional screen" come down before he has the impulse to bolt. But he admits that no matter how self-aware he becomes, he nevertheless will always have the impulse to leave when he gets "flooded." He knows he'll always be dealing with the impulse to hit and run. "It's like gambling," he says. "You get addicted to getting out of the jam, and so any potential jam—like life—prompts the impulse. Because there's an adrenaline rush involved—you sort of hate doing it because you know the 'down' that's coming afterward, and at the same time want to with all your heart and can't resist."

It becomes, in other words, no longer about love. Or about friendship. Or people with feelings. It becomes, and is, an addiction to leaving. Literally. Neurologically. The leaving becomes the hit for the Hit-and-Run Lover. And there isn't a strong woman alive who wants to take on a gambler or a junkie or a practicing alcoholic, not if she has a choice. The problem with this pathology is that there are no clues, not like a gambler's or a junkie's; you only know he's sick when he's gone and can't be reached.

Greg sent a note to Kristin about three months later. "I'm so sorry," he said. "I have no excuse. It was terrible of me." He followed the note with a call. "Can we talk?"

"About?" she said, resisting the urge to hang up but not wanting to talk.

"Us?"

"Unless you were hijacked, hit by a truck, or had a near-death experience, there's nothing to say. Maybe if you were actually dead, we could talk."

He laughed, and then, seeing a possible opening, stuttered and tried to win her with self-deprecation.

Kristin hung up. The man was neither hijacked nor hit by a

truck nor dead. Worse, he wasn't even so horrified by his own behavior that he could promise that he had a support team with guns
pointed at his head, not to mention a therapist and a cocktail of
medications, to ensure that he wouldn't do it again. He called his
love to say nothing other than that he was a victim of his own
love-destroying behavior and that she should understand, if she
would, that it was entirely possible that she'd became roadkill all
over again.

She only half expected him to beg her and promise her and feel
terrible and *do* something. "I was enough of a wimp to hear him
out, but all it did was remind me of what a disaster he was; that he
didn't comprehend what he had done and had the gall to want to
leave the door open to do it again! I wanted to say, 'What will you
give me if I take you back? A car? A new home?' Certainly this
wasn't about love, or caring."

And that's the whole point. The Hit-and-Run Lover offers little
sustenance to the people who love him and takes little responsibility
for his actions. I say "who love him" rather than "whom he loves"
because I question whether he feels love anymore. And I say "anymore" because he obviously once thought he was in love, but it
wasn't love, it wasn't even friendship, it was *idealization*, and he
loved putting the object, the icon, on a pedestal. But the icon, his
idol, wasn't real. He fantasized attaining this ideal but not inter-
acting with a real person. He's consummately, unutterably weak.

The Hit-and-Run Lover likes to fantasize about strong women
and to chase them. What he hates is to win them.

Telltale Signs of the Hit-and-Run Lover

1. **He comes on strong.** Even if his style is cool and his
method casual, he delivers a "Where have you been all my life?"

message. Instant infatuation is his game. He may be pushy ("What's stopping you? Just one cup of coffee! How bad could it be? Don't you need some caffeine?"), or he may be more furtive, attempting not to push or overwhelm you but instead to insinuate himself into your life (with those surprise sushi lunches). Either way, you get the feeling you don't have a choice: You're going to have to see him. He seems to have made a decision about you from the beginning—you're *it*—and he will get your attention. He may not call you to get it, or make plans; he's often subtler than that and sometimes even willing to go at your pace. But there's a certainty in his waiting: He's gonna getcha. And compared to this decisiveness, you feel ever so slightly pallid and vague.

2. He always approaches with gusto. Since he acts as if he knows something you don't (as if he gets it and you don't), there's a bullying quality to his insistence on the joys of "love": Why aren't you as in love with him as he is with you? Why can't you recognize what's good for you? Why won't you give him a chance? Why are you so afraid?

Why? Because you feel pressured, that's why. So you act a little stunned, a little vague, a little overwhelmed. "Why don't you get with the program?" he'll ask.

He wants to appear to be the perfect "catch"—even though you're not looking for one. It seems to offend him that you're not out fishing.

Correction: It's *especially because* you're not looking for a man that he's annoyed. Here's why: He knows, deep down, how profoundly unready he is for the kind of relationship he's trying to talk you into, so he goes to great lengths to appear super-equipped for it. Within a few hours of meeting him, you'll hear about the family he wants (if you're young) or the sexy plans for retirement (if you're not). You'll hear about the cleaner air he believes in, the lifelong monogamy he insists on, the fabulous lifestyle he envisions for the two of you. The dog, the cooking classes he's gone to, the wines he collects, the art magazines he subscribes to. You'll feel uncool.

What's he selling himself so hard for?

To prove that he is what he isn't.

Why isn't he asking anything about *you?*

Because you're incidental. This Drama King's drama is his own, like a mirthless standup comedian's. Remember, Drama Kings cannot and will not share the stage.

This man is not a grownup, he's a kid. He wants to chase you, not win you. If you return his passion, and his terror gets unleashed, then he will—yes, he *will*—bolt.

3. He makes you feel you should be less ambivalent. The lengths he goes to in order to make you see the light! To instill certainty! What he feeds on is the unrequited part of this, the fact that you're not so certain, not yet asking anything of him; not yet *in a relationship*. Your ambivalence actually turns him on. And as long as he's asking something of you and not the reverse, he'll be wild for you.

Myths about the Hit-and-Run Lover

1. He gave you enough signals; you should have been prepared. No, he didn't: You couldn't have been prepared. His departure was a natural disaster, a twister, an avalanche, and if it hadn't been an illness of yours that pushed him away, then it would have been the suggestion of a holiday or the discussion of a new home—anything that said "we." Carol recalled:

> *We were in a film class together at NYU, and we made wonderful, crazy films together. He was much younger—I never expected to have more than what we had in class, but then he was*

so aggressive. He kept asking me to go to movies after class or to rent weird foreign films or to go someplace where people we admire hang out.

I knew, once we did go to bed, that we were both having a fabulous time, that this was very much his doing, his desire. He was almost crowing at having proved to me how good it was. I never demanded anything from him—I let him control the timing, the place, everything. So I know it wasn't that he got scared because I expected too much or anything like that. I expected nothing. I was getting so much more than I'd expected.

And then he never came back. Not only never came back to me, never came back to class. I never heard from him again. I asked our professor where he was, and she said, "He dropped out. That's all I know."

2. His departure was unplanned. Regardless of the catalyst, his leaving was hardly impulsive. He made the decision at some point; he felt it brewing, the itch to ditch, and ever since, he's lived with that secret. Some Hit-and-Runs feel a sudden revulsion: You're the wrong woman. Others never consciously understand what's turning them off, but they do know the demands are too great, the sense of obligation too overwhelming. Being a Drama King means he can't express any of this, so he just kept his changed mind, his queasiness, his plan, to himself. But there's no question that he knew and rationalized his need to leave. And he knew, too, that no power on Earth could have stopped him. Or changed his mind.

3. You need "closure." Closure occurs in startling ways, but rarely by having a conversation with a person who summarily dumped you. This is not the guy for that chat—even if you could find him to have it.

If the Visitor thinks women are out to trap him, and the Proprietor thinks women are out to ditch him, the Hit-and-Run Lover simply prays that the ditch he's dug himself into won't ever be discovered. He arranges this with the skill of Osama bin Laden, finding a dank cave somewhere to go to ground in. Anyone who says, "We'll hunt him down! We'll find him!"—well, you know *that* story. You will deal with the hurt all alone. You will wonder whether, if you'd held on tighter, had married him quickly, had loved him more ferociously, he'd be there with you now. No. He'd be in a deeper ditch.

4. If he'd shared his panic, you could have helped him stay. No, no, and no. Like his namesake, the hit-and-run driver, he was able to smash into another human being and leave her like roadkill in his wake. That roadkill was you. This Drama King has ice, cowardice, and a horrifying lack of compassion at his core.

Why You Were Taken In

Because a man who woos you so dramatically is often irresistible. He seems to know something about love that you don't, something he wants to teach you, if only he can get you to care. And those sushi lunches and all the other signs of "caring"? So sweet. Those wonderful art-house movies he took you to, the tiny ethnic restaurants no one else had heard of that he knew the owners of. His attentiveness, apparent willingness, and that quirkiness that made him seem so wonderfully unconventional.

And, most compelling, his ostensible "Yes!" to you and to life.

What You Learned from Him

1. Compassion is more important than passion. Dr. Steven Stosny, who offers a program called "Love without Hurt: Compassion Power," believes that it is not love that abusive people lack but compassion for those whom they love. He defines compassion as the ability to sympathize with the hurt experienced by one's lover, combined with the desire to make it better. Failure of compassion, he says, can feel like abuse. If the Hit-and-Run Lover empathized with the hurt he might cause his lover by vanishing, he might be able to stop himself and to act with compassion instead. His failure to do so, combined with his lack of remorse and his decision not to make amends, are, alas, characteristic of Drama Kings' behavior, whether you dub it abusive or not.

2. If only you had . . . Stop. You were incidental in this drama. This particular Drama King thrived only on the *pretense* that he was capable of sustaining a good relationship. You were duped. The man is a love fraud.

3. A man who looks too good to be true probably is. And he's probably a Drama King. More lessons of the century.

Chapter Seven

Drama King #5: The Feeling-Impaired Guy (FIG)

Better to be without logic than without feeling.

—*Charlotte Brontë*, The Professor

All the Drama Kings we've seen so far—the Visitor, the Proprietor, the Easygoing Guy, and the Hit-and-Run Lover—distanced themselves from their feelings as well as their relationships by freaking out, zoning out, checking out, or not engaging to begin with. Whatever their detachment technique, however, they have felt *something* and communicated it *somehow*.

Meet Walter, the owner of his own graphic design firm in Knoxville, Kentucky. Walter was gorgeous. Dark, thick hair worn long, like a French schoolboy's, and ridiculously bright eyes that Jenna, his previous girlfriend, insisted were "cornflower" blue. He was thirty-five and single, married and divorced long ago—a "blip," he called that part of his life in his early twenties. He had the air of a deeply confident, competent man. He had hobbies and interests

153

and an adult, cultured life. And Jenna, his partner at the firm, fell madly for him.

> *Walter is a* grownup. *He has an apartment with a real working kitchen that he uses. He cooks—has parties and meetings in his home. He goes to the theater. He travels around the country to do fun things—to catch performances of Wagner or to see the Eagles when they came back together. He plays the banjo in a country band. He studies Greek. He loves his life, and I instantly wanted to be a part of it—the whole thing, not only the work part. I'd never met a man so mature and content, and I truly believed that if I could be part of his life, I'd be mature and content, too. I loved everything about him—his work, his talent, his home, his dog, his car, his wit: everything. He was a little cool, a little brittle, but I figured I'd soon change that if he let me in.*

Jenna broke a date with the man she was seeing—casually, she says—in order to go out with Walter the first time he asked her out, and then never went back to seeing that man or anyone else. After two dates with Walter, she couldn't imagine any other man. She was happy to have her work life and her love life filled with him. Within three months, she was living with this man she came to refer to as a domestic god.

Talented as she was, strong as she was, she was nevertheless clearly in his thrall. Walter, being quite perfect himself, also liked things at work and in his home to be perfect, and he made sure they were. His banjo was never left out of its case, nor were his CDs left out of theirs; the dishes were done as soon as they were used; the beds made in the morning before the coffee was. His neatness, the order that surrounded him, meant everything to him. Jenna was asked to take off her shoes when she entered the front door.

When she began staying at Walter's several nights a week (his place being where he was most comfortable), he began to get cranky. "Shh," he'd say when she came in late from work, "the dog's asleep." She'd find signs on the refrigerator: "Don't touch the tuna. It's for my lunch tomorrow." She had the sense that she was now a part of an ecological balance so delicate that her very breathing upset it.

Moreover, Walter was extremely complimentary of her half the time and extremely critical the other half. He'd be sweet to her in the evening, then chilly the next morning. He'd approve of her work one day, then pick at the same work the next. He'd look at her lovingly, then with frightening disapproval. She began to think his alternating moods might be calculated, a game to keep her on her toes.

Within six months, she hated the game. And she felt utterly disenfranchised from his home—as though she were such an over-whelming presence and incompetent housekeeper and cook that she should take some adult home ec classes. When she told him this, half kidding, he shrugged and agreed that the classes might do her some good. Not for a moment did he feel he was being hard on her or dismissive.

So here she was with this beautiful prince, feeling like Cinderella—permitted neither to do any sweeping nor to feel safely loved. They were lovers, yes, but when she omitted her desire for him from the equation, she realized the extent to which his be-havior toward her was mechanical. He went through the motions, but he didn't feel anything.

I realized that I was with a beautiful but icy human being, someone who cared so little about me that the only anxiety con-cerning me he ever expressed was when, say, I helped myself to food, and he feared I'd drop some on the floor. I told him I thought I'd better stay away from his house for a while—I only messed it up—and he said, "Good idea." Like that, as if he were on the phone with a new client, discussing new drawings for an ad campaign.

So I did it: I left him and never went back. I refused to see him socially. I had many clients of my own, so I continued working at the firm for another year, until I could find a better spot, but we never spoke again about dating.

I know he was stunned by my decision, because he tried all sorts of tactics to engage me again, but they were clearly strategies; there was nothing coming from his heart.

The Feeling-Impaired Guy (FIG) is the *reductio ad absurdum* of Drama Kings. He's smart and responsive, but his emotions can't be excavated from the core of his psyche, and so they never come into play. No one picks this up readily because he covers it well and because the depth of his chill is so unthinkable; so unlikely and inhuman. He's skittish but not sensitive. He doesn't display any apparent mechanism for protecting his feelings, perhaps because he senses that they're long gone, vanished like an early case of mumps or some other unpleasant childhood illness, never to show up again. He may be charming, ultracompetent and cool, like Walter, or dramatic and hot. The FIG comes in all types, but he always has an emotionally frozen core. The only tip-off? The chill you feel when you're around him. The brusqueness that comes through. The profound remove. His subtle mixture of grandiosity and disregard for others' feelings can seem at first like shyness. But as anyone who tangles with him discovers, whatever few feelings he has are reserved, when they come forth, for himself. They don't find their way over to the person on the other side of the bed.

All women feel lonely with Drama Kings. But the loneliest of all are with FIGs.

J im, the nattily dressed congressman of his state, hasn't heard a
word his beloved, Beth, has said since Bush the Younger took office the first time. "It's the weirdest thing," she told me, this woman
who, as chief spokeswoman for one of the political parties in her
state, was paid hundreds of thousands of dollars a year to speak to
adoring crowds. "Jim hasn't picked up on a conversation I've tried
to start in months."

She once sent him to an ear specialist to have his ears checked,
thinking that maybe the poor guy really *couldn't* hear and that his
familiar declaration, "Let's not talk about it right now," was just a
cover to save his pride. She read his willingness to go to the doctor
as a sign that maybe once the wax in his ears was cleaned out, he
would become less defensive about his true inability to hear and
therefore magically communicative. "Magical thinking," she now
says of her fantasy.

Communicating with a Drama King is not easy under the best
of circumstances, but it is hardest with the FIG, whose mottos—
"I don't want to hear it!", "I don't want to discuss it!", and "Conversation over!"—pretty much articulate his feelings about the
prospect of deepening a relationship through mutual understanding. He's often more passive than punishing, more detached than
cruel, and while he can be mild mannered and pleasant, actual emotional contact with him is slippery. It's quite possible that Jim really
hasn't listened to Beth since the day she said yes to going to bed.

Beth added, though, "He does hear compliments. He remem-
bers them and mulls over them and gets enormous pleasure from
them and cites them and can hear them repeated over and over. So
if you're willing to figure out new ways to tell him how fabulous he
is, he'll never, ever miss a word of it. It's hard to develop a conversation based on them, but you know what? It's all the conversation
he needs."

Characteristic of one kind of FIG is his way of bowing out of all conversation and not making any real moves in the relationship. If he's this passive type, he's easy prey for an assertive woman, because she must choose him. Although it sounds unlikely that any strong woman ever *would* choose him, many do, either to exercise their assertiveness skills or because they travel a lot and don't have time for anything that might resemble courtship.

"I didn't actively choose him, but he definitely kind of fell into it when I was around," said Brenda, an executive with a large coffee manufacturer, who went on to struggle with the definition of "it."

> *I mean, he never actively, and with sustained thought and interest and intention, chose to get involved . . . but then, I didn't really, either.*
>
> *We met at a zoning board meeting in our town. Someone was trying to build a McMansion in our tiny neighborhood on the river, and we'd both shown up to fight it. We were united in fighting the proposal, and so, after a few of those exhausting and emotional ZBA meetings, I asked him to come have a drink and maybe some pasta at my place—to clear ourselves of the homeowner's greedy plan but also to shake off the toxicity of the power-hungry board members themselves. He is an adorable guy—adorable-looking, that is—and we had this passionate cause in common.*
>
> *He was very depressed. Divorced, father of a teenage girl who won't talk to him because of the divorce. Ex-wife encouraging the kid. I wasn't eager to become a part of that triad, but we sort of fell together that night and a few times thereafter. Now he comes to me because, I think, I'm there. He doesn't hear me, and I don't think he sees me; he's too caught up in his misery and his terror of losing his daughter's love forever. If I weren't there, I imagine*

he'd stay home and lift weights. If I weren't there for a while—
say, three times?—he'd find another person to spend time with.
To him I am, excuse me, pussy—and no different from any other
pussy on the planet.

Brenda puts up with the casualness of it all, she says, because at the moment, she has time for little else if she wants to have anyone in her life at all.

The Feeling-Impaired Guy is often mistaken for a shy person who merely keeps his feelings to himself, or who has been hurt and can't quite commit fully again—or an aggressive workaholic type who never did the home thing very well. Sometimes he appears to be a Visitor—coming and going but not wanting to stay. He isn't. He wants to stay. He has few feelings, is all. Nor is he a strong, silent type who can't express himself but hides a world of deep feeling that will one day burst forth into connection. *This is what he seems like and often looks like.* But no, no, no, don't go by his looks. It's a grave mistake to ascribe depth to a FIG or to hope for hidden treasures beneath the cool, competent exterior. They aren't there.

The modern FIG sometimes comes in the form of an enlightened person: an evolved, sensitive, spiritual man who has simply meditated away all worldly aspirations for attachment. He may be a yoga master or a guru or a trainer or someone else who has had to work hard to master his emotions and to surrender his ego to get onto a spiritual path. These FIGs are the trickiest to uncover because lack of attachment to the worldly is precisely that to which they aspire, and mastering that detachment is, to them, a very good thing. But I've never met a FIG who is *truly* spiritual—only those who have managed to use their coldness and disregard for others to their own advantage. These clever souls have translated the spiritual idea of staying unattached—the notion of being a witness to one's emotions rather than a victim of them—into a comfortable detachment from everything and everyone. The distinction is subtle, but there is a chill to the latter, a self-involvement that is antithetical to true spirituality. The spiritual man is neither egocentric nor disaffected. The FIG is both.

Thus, a FIG may seem like a Zen master who believes in a new and healthy way of relating to others, but he is merely masquerading as a way of coping with his primitive absence of emotion. I've rarely met a FIG, in other words, who is truly evolved; rather, he is truly cold. We don't feel the chill as quickly as we would if we witnessed the same structure in a woman, because he is a man, and we respect autonomy and independence in men without challenging its costs to a relationship until—we're in one.

Brenda was twenty-six, and the feeling-impaired Drama King she met at the zoning board meeting, Allen, was thirty. At first she thought he was simply ill-bred when, after months of these zoning meetings and months of getting together afterward, she told him she'd wanted him for so long to come over to her in the mornings and just touch her.

Not for sex, just out of affection. It took a lot for me to say that. It was the truth. Hey, did I ask for marriage? For a baby? No. I asked to be touched. Simple, no? You know what he said? He said, "It would never occur to me." He wasn't intentionally being cruel; he was telling me what I already knew. He didn't feel the desire for connection, nor did he crave emotional contact, nor did he have the loving impulse to feel my skin or even to reach out and make me, his lover, feel good. Normal intuition, regular responsiveness: not there. He was like a robot.

He enjoyed sex, she said, if it was quick and lighthearted, like a game of gin rummy, in a kind of infantile way.

Nothing sophisticated, nothing textured or adult. Lots of black humor about men and women. Sex jokes you see on the Internet—you know, killer broads and gold diggers, and their brutalized husbands. That sort of thing.

Strangely enough, he's the most fun when he's shopping. He loves toys. Not for me, ever, but for him. He can bond with, say, a camera, or a car, more than with me.

"Do you even like me?' I once blurted out, trying to avoid asking whether he loved me, which I'll be damned if I'll do and don't even know why I'd want to, except I was feeling so deprived. But immediately, I felt clingy and pathetic and needy and wondered where my self-esteem had gone. Yet I couldn't stop. So I reframed the question. "We're sleeping together, right? And while you are under no obligation to love me, I thought perhaps you'd once in a while tell me what you do feel."

He looked pained and mumbled something about the fact that he did show up, after all. Like I should be grateful! I should read into that . . . what? Showing up is his greatest gift of intimacy, because it's so hard for him even to do that?

Pamela was married to a FIG, Doug, for four years.

The showdown came when I was crying in bed, lying next to him after my brother Matt died—a sudden, terrible death at 28 from an auto accident—and my husband would not respond. So I would get up and lie in the other room and weep. He would hope that my family wouldn't call me because we were all so deep in mourning it clearly upset me to talk with them, even though I wanted to. Doug hated me to be on the phone with them. He said, "It upsets you," but actually, I soon came to realize, it upset him.

For one thing, it pointed out whom I was confiding in; it illustrated who was giving me solace and who was not. That was what he didn't like: that although he wasn't helping, he wasn't the one I turned to. Mostly, though, these conversations made it clear that I was not available to be a wife—and I was supposed to be, regardless of whether he was acting as a loving husband. I was grieving. I wasn't on call.

So he would not respond to my pain, figuring, in his bizarre, passive-aggressive way, I guess, that I'd get over it sooner if I simply wasn't attended to. Can you imagine? Or that I was undergoing some process he needn't be involved in or in which he felt awkward participating. Whatever. It so hurt me that it broke my marriage right at the heart of it. And I said to him, "Doug, anyone would respond to a human being who is sobbing. Anyone would reach out. You don't have to be clever, you don't have to be smart, you don't have to have words. Why can't you reach out to me?"

And he said, "Well, you know, Pamela, it's been going on every day now for months and, well, I can hear you crying."

He had to get his sleep! *That was the bottom line.* My emotions were interfering with his schedule! *He even told me his work was being affected by my grief. And so I'd go into the other room and feel so alone I can't tell you. I can't explain it even now.*

My husband acted as if the inconvenience to him were intolerable.

I think of that word, *compassion*, and its root meaning—"to suffer with"—and wonder once again why it is that this quality is so lacking in Drama Kings, how they can be involved with someone and not feel sympathy for or protectiveness toward her. Sometimes I think the deficit lies in the caring part of the equation, sometimes in the dearth of compassion. Pamela concluded:

So not only did Doug fail, he didn't have any problem with failing; he thought I was asking too much or that I'd get over it. So I went to someone who didn't need to deny me my grief or debate whether he was getting enough attention or whether I'd had enough time to get over it—but who simply wrapped his arms around me. And I never went back home again.

I don't believe that the Feeling-Impaired Guys we're talking about here have the neuropsychological problems—mild autism, or Asperger's syndrome—that would warrant more serious concern. Nor do I think they're schizoid or sociopathic. Their disaffection falls just under the pathology mark—which is, of course, why they can pass as "normal" to strong women. Their behavior feels as if there are serious attachment problems, but not those that need psychiatric or medical attention. They are passive when it comes to a woman's needs, but they see to their own needs with vigor. They seem distant, but they attend to their own lives with the utmost intelligence, competence, and care. They still expect women to live entirely for them, even though when it happens, they don't like it.

It's not only sharing that's the problem, or caring, it's reciprocity, nurturance, involvement—that constellation of qualities we include under the rubric of "intimacy."

Here's another typical interaction with a FIG. Jackie was a software developer with Microsoft at only twenty-two. She'd been dating thirty-year-old Rick at her firm, a guy who just never said much, but gave up on him when he stayed too quiet for too long.

"Look, a lot of nerdy guys just aren't big on speaking a lot," she said. "I know that. I know them. I'm used to it. I'm pretty nerdy myself and don't speak all that much, either."

But one night, it got to be too quiet.

"Should we really continue seeing each other?" Jackie asked casually after a particularly pro forma round of sex.

"Sure," he said, smiling a sweet, vague smile. "Why not?"

She lost it.

"*Why not?* Because, you lumpen creature, not only do you not express how you feel, not only do you have no urge to express anything about your feelings, toward me or anything else, but you seem to have no feelings whatsoever. You seem impossibly disengaged."

"He thought about this for a moment," Jackie said. "He shrugged and, with an expression that looked so blank his features might melt right off his face, showed the usual: *nothing*."

It was then, at that instant, over. She looked at his vacant, expressionless, featureless face and "the whole thing, all of it, became clear. With his occasional fond smile and his distracted lovemaking, I had simply pretended I was getting enough sustenance—because that's what's out there in the mostly-boy computer world I live in. With my busy schedule, I kept saying to myself, his kind of male disconnection *worked* for me. I'm from the same mold they are. But no, I'm not, and now starvation gripped me. And I could no longer fool myself."

'Just one more thing,' I said, no longer afraid, no longer needing to hear anything satisfying but just expressing sheer curiosity. 'Have I made any impact on you? Has our time together had any meaning for you?' One look at his expressionless face, and I had my answer. It was scary."

Jackie got a card from the FIG she finally sent packing. It had a painting by Joan Mitchell on the front. He wrote, "The world was more colorful with you. Rick." It was the teensy nod, she felt, to the beauty he knew she offered and to his heartbreaking inability to share in it.

"So please, don't wrangle with the FIG anymore, okay?" I requested of Jackie.

She replied, "You mean, don't fight for deep feelings on some errant assumption that he has them? That they're down there somewhere where only I—wondrous creature, I—can excavate them? No, I won't. Finding the remnants would not only take a lifetime but prove what I already knew. I ran out of his life. He hardly noticed."

Telltale Signs of the Feeling-Impaired Guy

1. You may first ascribe his problem to being *hearing* impaired.

Often, a FIG really *is* hearing impaired, and I'm not sure of the reason for the correlation. But even if his hearing is fine, one significant tip-off to the guy is that he doesn't listen. Then you'll think he has attention deficit disorder, except that he can focus very nicely on pretty much everything he decides to—it's just that it won't be you. You'll go through a host of possible ailments that could explain his vagueness, his pleasant dissociation from you and your life, and none of them will quite explain it. That's because the only real diagnosis is that he's feeling impaired. You'll even attempt to explain it by thinking he's masochistic—that he needs extreme stimulation, more than the average person, just to experience sensory pleasure and pain. But that's not it, either. Face it: Nothing's gonna help.

2. Something crucial is missing in him. What's missing in the FIG is a deep, emotional vitality that we recognize as human, a protectiveness we associate with being male. He often just stands there numbly when something dramatic happens—you fall down, or the dishwasher explodes. "Dumbfounded" comes to mind, but "inadequate to the task at hand" is more likely. Or he will laugh, or joke, or leave. He really doesn't want to do whatever needs to be done. He doesn't really know what to say, either. Conversation becomes inadequate for connecting; words lose their meaning, and the emotions that prompt them have no value. But feeling impairment is part of the man. He lacks that primitive, unambivalent, unmistakably male urge to fix what's gone wrong or even to put his arm around you, both of which have the effect of feeding the female soul.

3. He doesn't attach. If the Visitor's attachment style is clearly both anxious and avoidant, the FIG's attachment style is more bizarre. It's nonexistent because he doesn't attach. He pretends to. He seems to. But he knows he can't, or won't (again, we're not interested in his precise psychology; that's for his shrink), so he goes along for the ride to try to convince you that he can—until it becomes too much for him. He volunteers a limb to the relationship, usually the one with the sexual-feeling centers in it, and succumbs to enough connectedness to gratify his simplest drives and his most primitive impulses. But he keeps his trunk and vital organs, his innards, his head and soul—and most certainly his heart—well out of reach.

4. He doesn't care much about others. He's usually been seriously burned—there's always someone, a mother, an ex, who did him in, someone whom he mentions and his face hardens or goes blank. And that relationship haunts and torments him. As a kind of balm, there's usually a dog or a horse or some other animal that he has bonded with and that seems to occupy the chief place in his heart. Sometimes there's a child he loves, but often when the child is older, the warmth between them diminishes. He sometimes is sort of close to a sister or one guy friend. But other than that, he has little need of human contact, makes very few emotional requests, and has ingenious theories to explain his rigidity and disaffection. He says he's an artist, a poet, a loner, a political anarchist, a Zen master. His theories always support his lack of feeling, presenting it as a good, even admirable and manly, thing.

One such man refused to give gifts for any reason whatsoever—not to a bride and groom, not to the mother of a new baby, not to his parents—because, he said, he didn't like to make people "have to feel grateful" or beholden to him. And he attributed his hatred of celebration to his hatred of the "bourgeois." As his girlfriend translated, "He didn't care enough about anyone to give her or him a present, and he hated celebrations because they elicited *feeling* when attended."

5. He believes love means never having to say you're sorry. Because he rarely feels bad, the FIG approves of his own motives and disaffection and doesn't feel much need to defend them. If you don't approve, he just accuses you of being ridiculously uncool. If he hurts your feelings, well, that's your problem. This is a way of controlling you through disconnection.

Myths about the Feeling-Impaired Guy

1. He's just shy. That may be, but it's an excuse for those who don't want to believe that he's so unbearably disappointing. People who claim that he's just shy (his mother, his grandmother) don't want you to leave, and they know you're going to.

2. "He hasn't found the right girl." Or, reworded, "He'll become attached to the right person; just give him time." It's unlikely—either the right girl or the time. He often isn't deeply attached to his parents or his children and wasn't attached to his first wife (or his second) or any of his girlfriends—so why would he start now? And how much more time do you want to give him?

Why You Were Taken In

He was cute—really cute. He was good-natured. He seemed more mature than other men. He wanted to fall in love, even though he never had before. Next time, of course, you'll ask yourself, "Why hasn't he?" He's *forty*. And you'll also ask yourself why you'd want to be the first person a man of forty falls for.

What You Learned from Him

You discovered that there is something more devastating for a man than performance anxiety, and it's the opposite: Being asked to be real, and *not* to perform.

As I said earlier, you learned that there are people other than sociopaths or those with medical and psychiatric disorders who don't feel very much, and people other than those afflicted with autism who have trouble attaching. That alone is a terrifying lesson, and it can mark the end of innocence more dramatically than anything else I can think of.

It's a hackneyed and outdated script, women's role with the FIG. Needless to say, it destroys the spirit to be in a relationship with someone so profoundly uninvolved that he can't distinguish you from all the other women on the planet; to realize for sure that he really doesn't *get* you. It's creepy and frustrating. Unfortunately, strong, beautiful, passionate women are often the ones who take the bait, either because they're so busy with other things or because they're intent on proving how lovable they are, intent on making themselves known, and become determined to break through to him. But truthfully, even a breakup won't faze him. In fact, it will relieve him. He will no longer be under pressure to feel something. "*Whew!*" is what he'll say.

In the FIG, some vital force that we might call core energy is missing—that male impulse to reach out and claim you for his own and to demand love for himself. I'm not speaking of sexual inadequacy here—FIGs can be sexually potent—but of a kind of life impotence, of emotional incompetence or unwillingness that creates a neediness in you that never existed before. It's as if they sense that they cannot meet their *uber*-adequate girlfriends on any common ground, and instead of rising to the challenge, they opt out. Their love is not just unrequited. It's nonexistent.

I want to emphasize once again that despite the differences among the Drama Kings, there are stunning similarities—the most pronounced being a deep-seated sense of inadequacy with women that they all glimpse in themselves but won't tackle, a longing for relationship but a refusal to ensure it, and entitlement to a kingly role that they know is vanishing. What ultimately disappoints strong women more than anything is not only being let down but also knowing that these men don't care; that they are missing and loath to develop the vital kind of strength it would take to *not* let them down.

Nevertheless, part of what accounts for the growing number of strong, happy women in the wake of such disappointing Drama Kings is their growing ability to reject being rejected; their insistence that love be a gift that cuts both ways. It offers something promising—but also something unstable, impermanent, elusive, explosive. Women know that love—with a Drama King, as with another, more rewarding man—is always a work in progress, an entity so constantly in motion and with such life of its own that it rarely can be counted on to stay the same, or stay at all. I now believe that growth occurs and strength flourishes in the most difficult, unsatisfactory, and temporary relationships just as they do in lasting, satisfying ones. The agitation, the pain, the "failure" of a relationship may well be stepping stones in the adult woman's growing understanding of herself and others, and in her quest for wholeness.

If you're just out of a relationship with a Feeling-Impaired Guy (or an Easygoing Guy, a Visitor, a Proprietor, or a Hit-and-Run Lover), I hope you'll call it a success because you learned from the experience, not a failure because you didn't see disappointment coming. I hope you'll say, "In that year, I learned what it felt like to be powerless, and I now feel empowered," or "I discovered crucial things about myself in that three-month relationship that I never could have in another, easier, longer one—and am twice the woman I was before," and "I learned that Drama Kings are wounded and damaged, but it's not my job to heal them," or "Next time, I want the intimacy I've worked for and that I deserve." By believing these affirmations, you entered the lives of Drama Kings a lover and exited a revolutionary.

Chapter Eight

"Why Do They Stay?"

When they are unhappy, women usually think they need more love, but the objective evidence suggests that they need more independence.

—*Historian Francesca M. Cancian,* Love in America

If you're still wondering why you and other strong women put so much time into doomed relationships with Drama Kings, why you and they don't pack their bags sooner, you're not alone. I'm asked the question all the time. "Why do strong women stay in relationships that drain and exhaust them? *Why don't they just leave?*"

Strong women stay in relationships with Drama Kings as long as they do—which isn't necessarily very long—because they want relationships. They love men and desire them. They want love. They want sex. They care what men think of them, and they want all the intimacy and involvement that partnership promises. They don't want to be alone. They know they live in a world still set up to be easier for couples than for singles. They hope that with increased commitment, time, and change, even rocky, weird, and dysfunctional relationships with Drama Kings can improve and develop into a new story, a narrative of deeper attachment, cooperation, intimacy, reciprocity, and continuing strength for them both. They're willing to work at it.

Sometimes they stay simply because they'd rather have a weird, rocky, and dysfunctional relationship for a while than have none. Everyone knows by now, since every developmental study shows us so, that girls and women flourish when connected to others and ensconced in relationships. So we women have a tendency to put enormous energy into our love affairs, sometimes overdoing it when our partners put in too little. Even the very strongest and most independent of us sometimes temporarily resort to the tactic of trying to assure a good relationship by using the old "feminine" conduct-book skills—accommodation, pleasing, deferring, silence, and, yes, manipulation—because, particularly with Drama Kings, it's the only way we can think of to have the sex and fun we want, the love and connection, and maybe marriage and kids, too. It's part of attaching to want to stay attached.

Strong women may stay longer than they planned to with Drama Kings because they don't respond to stress according to the well-known fight-or-flight model but to a newly articulated "tend-and-befriend" model developed by UCLA psychologist Shelley Taylor, PhD, and a team of colleagues. Noticing that almost all the studies on response to stress have been conducted on male animals who do illustrate the fight-or-flight paradigm, Dr. Taylor observed that the people she'd worked with for thirty years in her health practice do not. Women, she and her colleagues have speculated, respond to stressful situations by protecting themselves and their young (the "tend" part of the model) through nurturance and seeking support from others (the "befriend" part). Male dominance behavior seems to be involved with androgen hormones like testosterone, while female dominance appears to be linked to oxytocin, a hormone that actually inhibits aggression and fear and stimulates relaxation and the desire for social contact in survival situations as well as in breastfeeding, sex, and cuddling—the opposite of fight or flight!

So rather than leaving when things get tough, a woman's survival mechanism may prompt her to invest more energy in trying to connect or to stay put and increase her contact with friends—a possibility supported by research in humans and animals.

Stay put for a while, that is.

I have a better question for you, though. Why do women *leave*? All the women I interviewed for this book who'd been with Drama Kings left before the two-year mark. This is not the old story of men leaving women. This is not middle-aged husbands looking for younger women, not males fed up with "needy" women who they believe perceive them as meal tickets, not young men looking to have their cake and eat it, too, who are leaving in great numbers. Women are leaving *men*. Marriage statistics are telling: Two-thirds of all divorces are initiated by the wife! How could a truth that has so dramatically transformed our country's domestic landscape so elude the trend watchers?

When I reported the statistics a decade ago—after all, it's a fact I didn't make up; it's right there in government brochures—I was laughed at. I'd go on the air, disclose what women were saying, and then be asked the same old question even as I answered it: "So, then, if women are so unhappy, why do they stay?"

I'd repeat, "They don't. That's the point. They're walking out the door."

They still are today. As a result, much has changed. Married-couple households, which accounted for 80 percent of the population in the 1950s, now account for only 50.7 percent; married couples with children, once the cozy composition of almost all American households, now make up a mere quarter of them and will probably decrease to a fifth by 2010; families with husbands who make the money and wives who work in the home account for a measly one-tenth of all households. *These domestic changes were spearheaded by women.* One paper reiterating statistics about women leaving concludes, "While these statistics alone do not compel a conclusion that women anticipate advantages to being single rather than remaining in the marriage, they do raise that reasonable hypothesis."

As an American, a woman, and a wife, I wonder whether any other institution with similar cockeyed statistics could escape notice. If sixty-five percent of women schoolteachers fled the academy, or if the same number of female soldiers left the army, wouldn't the culture be alarmed? Wouldn't we start asking new questions instead of old, irrelevant ones?

If an exodus from any other treasured and important institution were led by one gender, wouldn't there be a serious national effort to discover what made them flee or to redress their grievances, find incentives to encourage them to stay? Women's wholesale retreat—from Drama Kings but also from other men—is all the more startling because relationships are the habitat in which so many young women believe they want to be, and marriage is the environment they grow up assuming will be the most nurturing. After all, ninety percent of American women marry at least once before their fiftieth birthdays, and they do so expecting to thrive—and intending to stay.

Here's another statistic: Single women are far less depressed than married women. And single men are far more depressed than married men. If many of these men are Drama Kings, then the group of people in our society who are most in need of the balm of intimacy are the least able to let it reach them.

At the time I first heard these numbers, I was interviewing married women, hearing so many of them struggle to articulate why they felt as disenfranchised or alienated in marriage as they might in an institution in which they're emphatically unwelcome, such as the Vatican. I remember thinking then that no billion-dollar initiatives "to support marriage" make sense unless it's clear what part needs support. What needs fixing in marriage is the same as that which needs fixing in relationships with Drama Kings: the part that isn't working for *women.* Men, far more often than women, thrive in marriage. Men, far more often than women, wilt and wither physically and psychologically outside of wedlock. It's men who find the institution of marriage to be the nurturant, comfortable place it's reputed to be for women—thus, it's men more often than women who remarry surprisingly quickly after they're divorced or widowed, and men, beneficiaries of the old system, who are not hurt by its inertia.

Marriage isn't just an institution, then, it's as male an institution as the NFL. And if marriage proponents really want to tackle the issue of why so many of the strongest women are hanging up their wives' uniforms years before crossing into the end zone, they had better take notice.

I've heard and read some of men's thoughts recently about this monumental social upheaval. In an article entitled "Middle-Aged Men Find That It's Cold on Mars," men married for many years admitted their astonishment when their middle-aged wives—that notoriously love-hungry and disempowered cohort—left them. The AARP study they were part of, which surveyed divorced men and women between forty and eighty, found not only that divorces were more often initiated by wives but also that the husbands never saw it coming. The women walked off without much talk or fuss. Often, they just quietly left. The study also found that men in midlife suffer more from separation than do women, who said that they weren't suffering at all; they enjoyed being alone.

Marshall Farr, a musician and cabinetmaker quoted in the story, revealed his shock at his wife's departure. "It was all set up," he said, as if he still couldn't believe it. "I liked what we had put together. Now I have to keep asking myself, 'What do I want? Who am I?'"

Another husband in the study, Chuck, a financial planner married for thirty-four years when his wife asked for a divorce, said, "Something was obviously going on, and I was either unwilling or too dumb to look at it."

Many young women who leave their relationships can't figure out why their unions made them so deeply, incurably uncomfortable. They'd say, "I'd wanted to be married all my life, so how come I couldn't make it work? How come I didn't feel like myself again until I was divorced?"

Searching for answers, sometimes they may see that they were in a no-win setup with a Drama King. But other times, they may blame the role of wife for their unhappiness. Like thirty-three-year-old Anna, a forensic psychologist divorced after a two-year marriage to a pediatrician seven years her senior, they say they couldn't cut it. "I was the wrong person for the job," Anna said. "I didn't like the personality I developed as a wife; I didn't like the person I became, or the way I thought."

Or they blame their former mates. Over and over again, I heard this refrain from not-so-gay divorcees like this twenty-nine-year-old president of a luxury leather goods firm.

> *I thought it was my husband I wanted to leave, not marriage itself—I believed that he and I just weren't a good team. It was only long after our divorce that I began to understand that the two of us probably had a negotiable relationship. What tore us apart was something else, something outside us, a third party we couldn't see or discuss, that seemed to be gnawing only at me— something negative I was experiencing and he was not. But it was fatal.*

Are you uncomfortable yet?

Nobody likes hearing about women who leave relationships, whether troubled marriages or troubled Drama Kings. Certain truths are just too painful, and this one is so scary we'd evidently rather deny it and divert ourselves with the wrong question.

Women have long been relied upon to stand by their men, so most people would far prefer hearing that *men* leave. It's as though some old, tragic story lives deep within us—a haunting but familiar and somehow reassuring narrative in which men are feckless and women faithful, men can't commit and women can, *men leave and women stay.* That tale has so long been thought to be the way of the world, it's as soothing as a lullaby. Which has more resonance, a story of a woman who disappeared and never called again or a story of a Drama King who disappeared and never called again?

We have well-worn, soothing supports in place for the latter scenario. "That bastard!" we say, comforting each other. "Men are such babies!" we agree, as though being lifelong partners with an infant were inevitable or okay. That four-fifths of the population no longer considers it okay is stunning to a culture that didn't see the last straw coming. Something chaotic inside us is triggered: What do we do now? Who's going to fix relationships if women don't? Will strong women leave not just Drama Kings but *all* men—leave them alone with their vulnerability, their hidden neediness and dependency? Women leaving men conjures up visions of pathos, social anarchy, moral bankruptcy, and, of course, Jefferson's fear for his daughter: spinsterhood. For if women really decide they don't need men to live happy lives, *what then?* What will they want? What will happen to love as we know it? What promise of comfort, family, children, will men have? The more conservative among us ask, Will women go wild without men to control them? How do we get women back where they were and make them the loving wives they're supposed to be? How do we make them *stay?*

Oddly, as women reveal what's next in our social evolution by forming unconventional relationships that suit them rather than society, as they luxuriate in a freedom they've never before experienced, and as they watch Drama Kings perform for a while and then leave the theater, the pretense grows that traditional marriage is doing better than ever. I've noticed a new frenzy to the age-old idealization of it: The more the U.S. Census observes the decline of married households and the triumph, in sheer numbers, of cohabiting and single men and women and other alternative intimate arrangements, the more the culture becomes misty eyed at the word *wedlock* (as long as it's heterosexual). The more it becomes clear that the nation's women are leaving not decades but just a few years after saying "I do," and the more strong women find joy and peace and fulfillment in their careers and their rich single lives, the more society perpetuates the joyous myth of happily ever after.

Why can't we get real? On the newsstands, in bookstores, denial inverts reality as magazines and how-to books reiterate the timeworn fantasy of connubial bliss, impervious to the data. There they go, like something out of the 1950s, relentlessly exhorting single women to hurry up and snag that balky bachelor, drag him to the altar before he runs away—scaring readers into finding matchmaking gurus, "womanly arts" teachers, speed-dating groups, dating coaches.

This flurry of advice becomes more strident, more relentlessly upbeat and insistent, in direct proportion to the number of women who are calling it quits and finding joy elsewhere. "Ten Surefire Ways to Make Him Happy!" the magazines promise—as if men's happiness, not women's, were the issue; as if pleasing a man were the answer to all relationship problems. Wrong again. Where are the advice mavens pressuring men to please women, urging husbands to nurture their wives, helping Drama Kings learn how to love? After all, whose pleasure is at risk? Who's *leaving?* Could it be that men, so contented in marriage, so soothed by relationship, don't want to think about their relational lives? Are some, like Drama Kings, so injured by disconnection that they perpetuate a rigid armor they don't want to break through?

Is it that women's pleasure, as a topic, is threatening—even taboo? Do they buy the cultural myth of men's independence, that men really *are* reluctant bachelors and don't depend for their deepest happiness on women?

That so many women of all ages are opting to be unattached—even when they never wanted to be, even when it's scary, even when women's standard of living is statistically likely to plummet—*that's* what the country should be talking about. Women's decisions to leave Drama Kings, to leave marriages—*that's* what it should be talking about. For the first time in our history, women don't need men for survival; they want them for intimacy. So they leave when they don't get it—and *that's* what the country should be talking about!

Tougher divorce laws? Laws that reverse women's right to control their own bodies? Advice to women to become kinder, more cheerful, more demure, more understanding, thinner, prettier? Forget it. Women aren't going back. Any conduct-book answers for happy coupledom that beat the same old drum, tediously adding more *shoulds* to women's lists, miss the point of who is dissatisfied, and—more important—reverses the problem of who'd better please whom.

Pleasing women: Where is that story? "Ten Surefire Ways to Make Her Stay!" "How to Have a Happy Wife: What Every Man Must Know!" "Secrets of Famous Woman Pleasers: How to Give Her More, More, More!" It's not as if women haven't volunteered an overwhelming amount of information to men about how to please them, but for the most part, men's magazines would rather go broke than run articles hinting at their readers' emotional vulnerability to women; editors would prefer to quit rather than suggest that their readers aren't sexual giants. The myth of men's psychological independence and God-given sexual prowess is as insistent as the myth of women's dependence and God-given nurturing skills.

If women's magazines have pushed self-improvement and the art of pleasing as the way to happiness, men's magazines sell entertainment, distraction, disconnection—making icons out of Drama Kings—and rubbing salt in the basic childhood injuries of both genders rather than healing them. A young male editorial assistant at a top men's magazine told me that he thought "relationships" was a legitimate topic for male readers—and, after he was hired, offered dozens of possible article ideas each week. Before long, he was chastised by the editor and publisher for "not understanding the

ethos" of the publication—an ethos he and several other staffers described to me as "half Mike Tyson, half Peter Pan."

Fight *and* flight. But in life, not in war.

As I watch one of the most dramatic walkouts ever, I think our society has a choice: either to go on ignoring it and continue to
rehash misty-eyed myths that encourage strong young women to
race into relationships, only to flee them like horses from flaming
barns, or to help these women create an environment where they're
less likely to get burned. We can rail against women who leave—or
embrace their insistence on an extreme makeover of the man-
woman bond. We can go on pretending that marriage is the place
women love and men leave, or heed what women declare they want
in their unions and help them get it. We can belittle strong
women's new role in the world and strong men's new role in relationships, or honor and support both. We can urge women to excuse, analyze, stand by, and dutifully applaud a Drama King, or
cheer them on in their unprecedented decision to move on.

Chapter Nine

When the Curtain Falls

Not to discover weakness is
The Artifice of strength

—*Emily Dickinson*

"**B**efore I turn 67—next March—I would like to have a lot of sex with a man I like. If you want to talk first, Trollope works for me." So said the ad a woman named Jane placed in the *New York Review of Books* in the autumn of 1999. It made me happy, not just because of its author's candid request for sex and plenty of it, not just because of her humor and her age, but because of her obvious high spirits. Subverting the romantic script women are thought to want—the moonlight walks on the beach, the fuzzy talk-to-me-first-and-then-we'll-see foreplay—she sent a new message to men that has since become the mantra of older and younger women alike: I'm already all ready; no sweet talk needed. Goodbye to the ancient men-want-sex, women-want-relationship paradigm. Enter a paradigm of pleasure, in which men and women want both sex *and* relationship.

The evolution of strong women has brought them to this paradigm. Women are playing, learning, looking out at love and life from their own eyes rather than viewing themselves, judging themselves, through others'. If they don't like what they see out there in the frozen, stymied, wounded hearts of Drama Kings, the transformation from object to subject is nevertheless dazzlingly life changing. Deflecting what has long been referred to as the male gaze and gazing back without fear has enabled women to take charge of their own pleasure and to control their own destinies. This new wholeness has made their dealings with men increasingly honest, authentic, daring, and caring. And though these dealings are fouled up by Drama Kings temporarily, women quickly take their strength back. They're saying, for the first time in history, "If I have to choose between myself and relationship, then I choose myself!"

Women know the weird bargain that men and women struck when men's power was funneled into the workplace and women's into the home. Women know their "strength," then, lay in their ability to suffer dishonesty and pretend it was okay, to please and "influence"men to get what they needed. They know that such handling of men was manipulation and that men alternately suspected and succumbed to it. They know they're not innocent in the deal they long ago struck with men, but they've admitted it, discarded it, and even if vestiges of that bargain still remain, they find it increasingly repugnant. Women know that the price that they paid for this sad subterfuge was men who settled into a fuming silence, born of distrust of women's true motives and feelings and their own inability to change men's need for real connection. They know the rage and depression at having been deprived of so much of their strength, and men know it, too.

What kinds of love relationships *could* couples have had then, with so much anger, guilt, and falseness in their dealings with one another?

In the world of mating, the cultural crises are daunting—the end of courtship, the new meaning of forever, the waning of male initiative, and the sheer difficulty of finding a man to love and marry at a time in life when one is ready. And so are Drama Kings, with their disconnection, detachment, their denial of their need for relationship and their dependency on women, their inhibited sexual desire—their determination to treat love as if it were a performance and only they were on the stage. They may be heirs or penniless; have noble intentions or no intentions; be kind or cruel, powerful or passive. Many of them appear to be good men. They may *be* good men. Until they become mates. Or even dates.

But they're not fatal; they're mere stumbling blocks. Armed with increased personal power and love of their own lives, women overcome these obstacles with new optimism and a new willingness to write unconventional stories with their lives. They know that Drama Kings are merely a learning experience, and a good one. They're embracing what they've learned from them and, knowing they deserve better, are going out and getting it.

No Mr. Darcy? No Mr. Right? No Mr. Perfect? Then a woman will take some downtime, alone, in her own home. Or at work. Or with her friends. Or her dog, books, skis, boat, climbing gear. She is no longer trying so hard to please, to be perfect. She is trying, to paraphrase pediatrician-turned-analyst D. W. Winnicott—who urged women to loosen their aspirations enough to be "good-enough" mothers—to become a good-enough woman. And when Mr. Good Enough, a guy willing to confront his wounds and re-learn the skills of connection and relationship, shows up, she will confront *her* own wounds, the ones that have kept her silent in relationship. She will reach out. She will speak out unafraid. And, encouraged by her, so will he.

She'll have a gut feeling: Can this man connect? Does he listen? Is he interested? Does he seem threatened? Does he bring up the future in ways that don't seem as if it's a fairy tale—and at an appropriate time? Does he seem open to sharing? To love?

Nobody is claiming that all this is easy. There's a catch to growing strong. As one woman put it:

> *The story peeking through in my daydreams is always something out of Jane Austen, a neat, happily-ever-after scenario. These stories still haunt me. Even when I'm off on assignment alone, living out my dream of adventure, the "ending" I keep going back to in my head is the part where I'm done and the story ends. Where my life is simple; neatly tied up and I'm saved by some guy.*
>
> *I can't tell you how hard I fight against this ancient urge to hurry up and reach that place where Mr. Darcy comes in. Here I'm striving to enjoy the quest, to write my own story, to revel in the process, thinking now is the best time in my life—when boom! I'm suddenly thinking "I'm getting old! I should settle down! It's now or never!"*

They're living lives that Elizabeth Bennet, saved from poverty and social ruin by Mr. Darcy, would have given anything for. But as joyous as having a new story is, they know the new plot is complicated and its ending often unusual and unplanned and unconventional.

Love's outcomes are no longer guaranteed. Forever seems to have been replaced by *whatever*. Strong women may not meet the men they want at the time they're ready. In my generation, women in love struggled to have the career they wanted; today's career-minded young women are struggling to have the love they want. In the place of the familiar happily-ever-after stands a never-before, lawless frontier filled with frightened Drama Kings. New and un-conventional love stories are emerging, with new heroines, new plots, new arrangements, and a new order of masculinity and femininity.

For the first time in history, middle-class women do not need men in the traditional ways—for safety, for money, for a life. So they're demanding instead what they always wanted but couldn't ask for: emotional connection, presence, intimacy. Sex with enough foreplay, enough seduction, enough closeness, to please *them*. Men are baffled not only because the needs they are being asked to fill differ so from what their fathers and grandfathers understood to be their jobs but also because full-fledged intimacy requires strengths and skills in love they've never learned. Moreover, as we've seen on these pages, they are strengths and skills that were once left solely to women: Men didn't have to develop them. This maturational mismatch may be contributing to an increasing distrust among lovers of all ages.

Some say young women expect too much now; they're too en-titled, too blunt, too demanding—insisting as they do on sex *and* love; a nurturant man *and* an old-world provider; independence *and* intimacy. They're accused of outrageously upping the ante, piling on more loony hopes for the kind of gauzy, cartoonish intimacy that's impossible to deliver and ridiculous to want. If they'd just lower their expectations of love and of men, they'd be happier.

Lower expectations? A bad strategy. Just as I found in 1992 that women who said they married in order to have fun actually *had* more fun in their marriages, Donald Baucom, PhD, of the University of North Carolina, studied couples' expectations of each other and found that people with the highest expectations of their mar-riages most often have the highest-quality marriages. By extrapo-lation, lowering expectations merely increases the probability that a woman will get a Drama King . . . in perpetuity.

Women, who have a far more practical, less romantic view of relationships than men do, and who fall in love less often than men do, say they want honest, loving connection. A woman, in my experience, wants a man who doesn't want to control her; who gives her the same psychic space and freedom he asks for; who is willing to give up old gender roles; and who revels in her strength as she revels in his. A man willing to fit into and honor her complicated life, as women have long fit into and honored the lives of men. A man who wants to please and know her, as she has for so long wanted to please and know men.

This desire for intimacy is not a female-only desire. It's what infants of both genders come into the world hardwired for: an old, deep need rooted in a time when our attachments were crucial to life. Intimacy is what children of both genders desire. And intimacy is what adults of both genders (whose childhood wounds of disconnection have been healed) want, too.

Drama Kings, the walking wounded, go on thwarting intimacy, sadly creating drama by substituting lonely star performances for intimate duets. But while they go on shutting down and holding out—withdrawing, withholding, and pushing away; letting women act out all their dependency needs while at the same time deriding them for being so sensitively caring—other men are changing their tack. Why? To try for the lasting love that is the hope of men and women alike, to make that elusive "forever" happen.

I've found this male yearning for connection expressed in an unlikely place: country music. Unlike rock or soul, which even in the '60s had Aretha and Tina and Janis demanding respect and sex, and Smoky and Marvin and Otis offering sweetness and tenderness and healing in return, country songs have long kept intact a bad-man/good-woman paradigm straight out of the conduct books of two centuries before. Tales of good-hearted women and their two-timin' men, women who'd stand by their cheatin' guys, and men who hung out in bars with other men's wives—that was the formula. Women waiting at home and men feeling guilty but free in bars and trucks—that is what country music has been about.

But of late, male country singers are crooning a different tune. I'm hearing a plea neither for forgiveness nor for just one more chance, but rather for the chance to revive the old definition of forever—the one that meant . . . forever. The tune that soared to the top of the charts in 1999 was Kenny Chesney's "How Forever Feels," in which a *man* wishes for lasting love. And the number one song of the entire decade from 1990 to 2000 was "Amazed," by Lonestar. It, too, was about the transformation of a man who finds closeness with a woman and, surprised, finds he wants to spend the rest of his life with her. This new spin suggests that, as prosaic as these sentiments are, they don't come easily today. Men and women want to fall in love as much as they always did, but staying together is so much less likely than it once was. Drama Kings, I think it's clear, are least likely of all to ever sing a duet.

To make that happy ending really happen, men have to be willing to connect. They have to be willing to become relationally strong, which means having the courage to be vulnerable. A love that lasts doesn't come about naturally anymore (if it ever did), and it can no longer be forced by custom and law. It can only be *made* as a real relationship.

I see these men making real love all around me: men who are up all night with the kids and doing the laundry the next morning before going to work; men who see the pressure their lovers and wives are under and who can take over the relationship-maintenance job—not as a favor, not to "help out" because they've got to, but as a way of embracing fully their new role. These are men who shrug and say, "She's stressed, kids, let's let her sleep," or "Here's what needs to be done around here—and I'm going to do it" In effect, they're saying, "I may not know what this relational strength thing is all about, but I'll do it!" without looking beleaguered and resigned and victimized—and humiliated. As Dr. John Gottman, emeritus professor of psychology at the University of Washington, observes:

> *I believe the emotionally intelligent husband is the next step in social evolution. This doesn't mean that he is superior to other men in personality, upbringing, or moral fiber. He has simply figured out something very important about being married that the others haven't—yet. And that is how to honor his wife and convey his respect to her. It is really that elementary.*

Whether cohabiting or married, women—and some pioneering men—are attempting to create something new: big, roomy relationships that can later become big, roomy marriages that will house strong women in their entirety. They're getting rid of the old architecture of relationships, with its too-low ceilings, old-fashioned wiring, and uselessly outdated appliances. They're enlarging the very structure of their own relational "homes," adding new rooms for more psychic space and making the rooms that exist more nurturing and hospitable for themselves as well as for their men and children. Even if both genders find that walking this unworn path requires bravery and ingenuity and that writing their new love story requires imagination and fearlessness, they also feel gratitude to one another for the blessed freedom from the tyranny of the old paradigm.

In this Copernican moment, this welcome end of the man-centric world and the end of women's obsession with pleasing, many men are admitting (unlike Drama Kings, who just fake it) their bewilderment at the task ahead of them. Some feel overwhelmed. They ask, "Why wasn't I taught to honor a woman, respect her; taught to please her in the first place? Why do I have to learn it now, when women think I'm hopeless, when I was given none of the skills they so value?"

Their bafflement shows up everywhere. In a recent issue of *Men's Health* magazine, the blurb for a piece entitled "Babes in Boyland" reads, "Women are charging out of college, determined to take on the world—with or without a guy at their side, even when the time comes to raise a family. Are men prepared to meet the challenge?" And in the same issue, the editor asks, "If it's not a home and a paycheck that women want from us, what do we have to offer?"

I have the answer: What women have always offered men. What women have always wanted from men. Real intimacy. *And the relational strength it takes to create it.*

To be willing to offer that kind of strength, though, men will first have to learn to respect it. To respect it, they have to see its role in their own happiness and to understand and experience the pain and repercussions of its absence. Finally, they must see relational strength as a human strength, not a feminine one. They will have to want it as much as they have traditionally wanted worldly strength. Then they'll have to learn it—from women and from a culture that expects them to learn it, just as it has come to expect women to acquire worldly strength.

Rather than taking the position that women have gotten out of hand and need to back off from what they're asking for, Boston family therapist Terrence Real echoes his women clients' insistence, and says to the men in his practice, "Guys, this will *not* kill you!"— and then proceeds to help them do what they need to do.

> *Here's your choice: You can dig in your heels, and you can not meet her demands, and you will get more of what you've been getting. Or, you can take her seriously, figure out that part of being a man is not doing whatever the hell you want whenever the hell you want it, but part of being a good man is listening to the people that you love and actually trying to do some work on yourself to be more pleasing to them. And if you can redefine what being a man means to you . . . then I can promise you a happier, warmer, sexier, more loving Her.* Which door do you want to go through?

Real has also changed his approach to couples therapy. His training, like mine, taught neutrality: Thou shalt not take sides. So our work with couples usually goes back and forth, with the therapist at the helm, and, as Real puts it, we sound like this: "What do you think, Mrs. Jones? What do you think, Mr. Jones? Now what do you think about what he just said, Mrs. Jones?" And so forth, with the therapist giving no hint as to his or her position.

Real's Relational Recovery Institute has recently begun to shun neutrality, to break the taboo against taking sides. He knows that empowering women—first, before anything else—is the first step in ending their historical, culturally endorsed tendency to allow their partners to avoid developing relational strength. "We sound like this," he says.

> "*What do you think, Mrs. Jones?*"
> "*Okay. Mr. Jones? She's right. Now, here's what's going to happen if you shape up, and here's what's probably going to*

happen if you don't. Will you let me help you? This is not your fault. This is not a personal dilemma. This is not about your issues with your mother. This is about changing times."

You have not wasted time in relationships with Drama Kings but, on the contrary, have developed steadily, cumulatively, through them and because of them. It's as if the adult woman's self grows more resilient, durable, strong, through even the knottiest, nuttiest relationships—just as the child's self does. No kid gets to the adorable threes without passing through the terrible twos. No woman, I believe, gets to adulthood, after years of dating—which, after all, now begins at age fifteen—without grappling with a Drama King or two. Development through difficulty makes sense. Developmental theorists such as Margaret Mahler and John Bowlby stress attachment as the key to a child's development. Object-relations theorists, too, stress the importance of relationships in infants, and children's emotional and psychological growth. But Heinz Kohut, father of self psychology, went further than those who believed that parental love and nurturance—the good stuff of relationship—were the only keys to development. He pointed to the actual stress, pain, and conflict inherent in relationships with caregivers—a process he called optimal frustration—as integral to a child's growth, conceptualizing the self not in isolation but as a lifelong sequence of changing "selfobject" relationships. He believed that it is a combination of gratification and frustration *over time* that helps the child's self move forward to maturity and self-development. And Erik Erikson, in discussing the achievement of identity in his Life Stages theory, suggested that young women don't fully develop their identities in late adolescence and early adulthood, as he believed men do, but later on, in—yes—the context of intimate relationships.

Modern theorists such as Jean Baker Miller, MD, of the Elizabeth Stone Center for Developmental Services and Studies, and Carol Gilligan, PhD, have gone on to illustrate that both girls and women develop in a maze of relationships and that it is through this "growth in connection," as Dr. Miller puts it, that they thrive and mature. Dr. Miller calls her theory of women's development "self-in-relation" to emphasize how indispensable relationship is to women's growth.

It's as though the developing personality, all throughout life, is like kindling, needing to rub against another personality to create the spark that ignites the ever-growing self. For the self to become strong over time—and it does take time—it seems to need to get burned a few times by the fires of connection.

I sometimes wonder whether Drama Kings, such old-fashioned performers, were raised by parents who made it too easy for them relationally, sparing them this crucial, good friction—and indulging their Lone Ranger fantasies of autonomy. I've noticed that the young woman who finds the right guy early in life has only one disadvantage: She often must turn that good relationship into a difficult one at some point in order to find that friction that will rub her the wrong way—so she can grow strong. I'm suggesting that through a relationship with a Drama King (or two or three), a woman works out her own protean character, continuing to put together the residual fragments of self, recognizing and integrating past losses—and arriving as the mistress of her own well-being, the agent of her own pleasure.

"I'm not married yet," a thirty-eight-year-old woman told me. "I got all weird about that a few years ago, and then I realized that a lot of people aren't married yet, either. Or are on their third marriages! Meanwhile—and this will sound even weirder—I'm married to life. My mom looks at me and all my friends and shakes her head proudly and says it's so great that we've got such rich and varied lives. And we do."

One can go, as Jane (the woman who placed the ad) did, from the wounded, inebriated, and overweight wife of an argumentative bully—a quintessential Drama King—to the joyous 72-year-old who told Alex Witchel in a *New York Times* article that she turns down marriage proposals from men she meets on the Internet because "I'd have to give up the others then. I'd have to give up too much." Equipped and enabled at last to judge who might be the right partner and what kind of balance works for her in a relationship, Jane finds the answer to be, for her, no one partner at all.

The idea that her multiple relationships are failures or a waste of her time when they end is not for her. By this measure, how few relationships would count as successes! The assessment of the rightness of a relationship by its longevity is not for her. We can no longer continue to measure the success of a relationship by whether it lasts, for by that criterion, half of all marriages and an incalculable number of love affairs would be perceived as failures.

Jane had said that if a potential lover wanted to talk, Trollope would do. And I think if she ever found a guy she wanted to do more than hook up or hang out with, a guy to settle in with and love, a guy to consider "forever" with, Goethe would be her man. He's the one who said, "At the moment of commitment, the universe conspires to assist us."

Our attraction to Drama Kings may be hardwired, a built-in responsiveness to different types of familiar, traditional, masculine guys—an instinctive receptivity that doesn't weigh in their appropriateness for us. Some of these men are so cute and charming at first that, like the preloaded software that came with your first laptop and seemed to be hot at the time, it takes a while to see that they're so outdated they do little but take up needed space on your hard drive.

One day, you, like a brand new laptop, won't even recognize their programs. I hope this book makes that point clear and that it helps you stay on the path to becoming ever stronger, ever more your true self, ever more free of anyone who drains and exhausts you—until you wake up one day, full of energy and hope, and realize that Drama Kings no longer appeal to you, nor does any relationship that drains your strength. At that point, you will never again care to be with anyone who makes you choose between having your strength and having a relationship. When your instinct for happiness develops so far beyond what you were programmed to want that you truly don't want it anymore, you will have taken a magnificent, life-changing, evolutionary leap. And so will all the women around you. And Drama Kings will then become bit players with neither a stage nor an audience.

The men you will then find will be taking the same evolutionary step forward; they will be men who see the same possibilities in relationships that you do, and men who not only want and welcome what a strong woman offers but also find it just as pleasurable to give her what she needs.

I try out Thomas Jefferson's words—remember? The ones to his daughter, Martha, about the importance of pleasing her husband—on a twenty-five-year-old woman sitting next to me on the train, to see if they make any sense to her. I wonder how she'll respond to the urgency of a frightened American father so many years ago. The woman's name is Nancy, and she tells me she's just out of a relationship with a "cute" but apparently overweight and insecure man (who sounds to me like a very passive EGG), a man she calls "the original sports-watching, beer-drinking couch potato."

We talk about the men we now see on television, the men in sitcoms, the men who suddenly have less in common with Big on *Sex and the City* and more with adolescents at an overweight boys' camp—Drama Kings who go beyond being afraid of commitment and are neither physically nor emotionally equal to the attractive and strong women we're to believe love them. If men are unhappy about the way women speak of them, if they are concerned about male bashing, they should ask *male* writers not to portray men as incompetent, unwilling, and immovable, I suggest. "Yeah," she says. "Why must we turn on the tube and see darling, strong women and gross, weak babies for men?" Neither of us had the answer.

"What do you think this means?" I ask her: " 'The happiness of your life depends now on continuing to please a single person; to this all other objects must be secondary.' "

She takes her time before answering. "I think it's a woman who said it," she says softly. "She's saying that if I want to be happy, the person I should be most worried about pleasing is me."

Selected Bibliography

Ackerman, Diane. *Deep Play*. New York: Random House, 1999.

Allen, Douglas W., and Margaret F. Brinig. "These Boots Are Made for Walking: Why Most Divorce Filers Are Women." *American Law and Economics Association Review* 2, No. 1 (Spring 2000).

Armstrong, Alison A. *Keys to the Kingdom*. Sherman Oaks, CA: PAX Programs Inc., 2003.

Behrendt, Greg, and Liz Tuccillo. *He's Just Not That into You*. New York: Simon Spotlight Entertainment, 2004.

Benokraitis, Nijole V., ed. *Feuds about Families*. Upper Saddle River, NJ: Prentice Hall, 1999.

Conlin, Michelle. "The New Gender Gap." *Business Week*, May 26, 2003.

Dafoe Whitehead, Barbara. "The Plight of the High Status Woman." *Atlantic Monthly*, December 1999.

———. *Why There Are No Good Men Left*. New York: Broadway Books, 2003.

Douglas, Ann. *The Feminization of American Culture*. New York: Farrar, Straus & Giroux, 1998.

Dowd, Maureen. "Incredible Shrinking Y." *New York Times*, July 8, 2003, late edition, sec. A: 21.

———. "Men Just Want Mommy." *New York Times*, January 13, 2005, late edition, sec. A: 35.

Duffy, Peter. "I, Breadwinner?" *Village Voice*, December 21, 2004.

Dutton, Donald G. *The Abusive Personality*. New York: Guilford Press, 2003.

Enright, Elizabeth. "A House Divided." *AARP the Magazine*, July/August, 2004.

Epstein, Daniel Mark. *What Lips My Lips Have Kissed*. New York: Henry Holt, 2001.

Fels, Anna. *Necessary Dreams*. New York: Pantheon, 2004.

Fishman, Pamela M. "What Do Couples Talk About When They're Alone?" *Women's Language and Style*. Douglas Butturff and Edmund L. Epstein, ed. Akron, OH: L & S Books, 1978.

Garder, Ralph, Jr. "Power Wives." *New York Magazine*, November 17, 2003.

Gilligan, Carol. *The Birth of Pleasure*. New York: Vintage, 2003.

Glenn, Norval, and Elizabeth Marquardt, team leaders. *Hooking Up, Hanging Out, and Hoping for Mr. Right—College Women on Dating and Mating Today*. New York: The Institute for American Values, July 26, 2001.

Golden, Stephanie. *Slaying the Mermaid*. New York: Crown Publishing Group, 1998.

Goodrich, Thelma Jean, ed. *Women and Power*. New York: Norton, 1991.

Gottman, John M., PhD, and Nan Silver. "The Seven Principles for Making-Marriage Work." New York: Crown Publishing Group, 1999.

Gross, Jane. "Middle-Aged Men Find That It's Cold on Mars." *New York Times*, July 22, 2004, sec. F: 1.

Gurley Brown, Helen. *Sex and the Single Girl*. New Jersey: Barricade Books, 2003.

Hacker, Andrew. *Mismatch*. New York: Scribner, 2003.

Hanauer, Cathi, ed. *The Bitch in the House*. New York: HarperCollins, 2002.

Heilbrun, Carolyn G. *Reinventing Womanhood*. New York: Norton, 1979.

Hillman, James. *The Force of Character and the Lasting Life*. New York: Ballantine Books, 1999.

Jackson, Helene, ed. *Using Self Psychology in Psychotherapy*. Lanham, MD: Jason Aronson, Inc., 1993.

Kamenetz, Anya. "Superwoman 2.0." *Village Voice*, December 21, 2004.

Kramer, Peter D. *Should You Leave?* New York: Penguin Books, 1999.

Layton, Lynne. "Relational No More: Defensive Autonomy in Middle-Class Women." J. A. Winer and J. W. Anderson, eds. *The Annual of Psychoanalysis*, vol. 32. Psychoanalysis and Women. Hillsdale, NJ: The Analytic Press, 2004.

Lear, Jonathan. *Open Minded*. Cambridge, MA: Harvard University Press, 1998.

Macko, Lia, and Kerry Rubin. *Midlife Crisis at 30*. Emmaus, PA: Rodale, 2004.

Moore, Thomas. *Soul Mates*. New York: HarperCollins, 1994.

Morris, Betsy. "The New Trophy Husband: Who's Behind Every Powerful Woman?" *Fortune Magazine*, October 14, 2002: 79.

Nolen-Hoeksema, Susan. *Sex Differences in Depression*. Stanford, CA: Stanford University Press, 1993.

Norton, Mary Beth. *Liberty's Daughters*. New York: Cornell University Press, 1996.

Pals, Jennifer. "Identity Consolidation in Early Adulthood." *Journal of Personality* 67 (1999): 295-329.

Person, Ethel S., MD. *Feeling Strong.* New York: William Morrow, 2002.

———. *The Sexual Century.* New Haven: Yale University Press, 1999.

Popenoe, David, et al. *Promises to Keep.* Lanham, MD: Rowman & Littlefield, 1996.

Popenoe, David, and Barbara Dafoe Whitehead. "The State of Our Unions." *The Social Health of Marriage in America.* New Brunswick, New Jersey: National Marriage Project, 2001.

Real, Terrence. *How Can I Get Through to You?* New York: Fireside, 2002.

———. *I Don't Want to Talk about It.* New York: Simon & Schuster, 2000.

Roberts, Brent W., Ravenna Helson, and Eva C. Klohnen. "Personality Development and Growth in Women Across 30 Years: Three Perspectives." *Journal of Personality* 70: 1 (February 2002).

Robinson, Jane. *Women Out of Bounds.* San Francisco: Carroll & Graf, 2003.

Rose, Elaina. "Elaina Rose discusses new data which shows highly educated women are more likely to marry," interview by Bob Edwards, *Morning Edition,* National Public Radio, April 1, 2004.

Sargent, Greg. "Husband Hunting." *New York Magazine,* June 7, 2004.

Schwartz, Pepper. *Love between Equals.* New York: The Free Press, 1994.

Shapiro, David. *Neurotic Styles.* New York: Basic Books, 1965.

Slung, Michele. *Living with Cannibals and Other Women's Adventures.* Washington, DC: National Geographic Society, 2000.

Steinem, Gloria. *Moving Beyond Words.* New York: Simon & Schuster, 1994.

St. John, Warren. "In an Oversexed Age, More Guys Take a Pill." *New York Times,* December 14, 2003.

Tiger, Lionel. *The Decline of Males.* New York: St Martin's Griffin, 1999.

U.S. Census Bureau. "Americaís Families and Living Arrangements, 2000." Washington, DC: Governement Printing Office, 2001.

Viorst, Judith. *Imperfect Control.* New York: Fireside, 1998.

Watters, Ethan. *Urban Tribes.* New York: Holtzbrinck, 2003.

Winnicott, D. W. "Aggression in Relation to Emotional Development." *Collected Papers: Through Paediatrics to Psychoanalysis.* New York: Bruner Mazel, 1984.

Witchel, Alex. "Sex and the Single Senior." *New York Times,* April 7, 2003.

Index

A

Abuse
  from failure of compassion, 151
  hidden, 91
  learned helplessness and, 92
  from pathological jealousy, 85
Accomplishments, of modern women,
  12–14

B

Baucom, Donald, 187
Blaustein, Alvin, 111
Bowlby, John, 193

C

Choices, of modern women, 17–18
Compassion, failure of, in abusive
  relationships, 151
Conduct books, 19–20, 21
Conversation, gender differences in
  initiating, 52–53
Country music, male desires expressed
  in, 188–89
Courtship, disappearance of, 35, 38, 39

D

Dating, disappearance of, 35, 39
Depression
  in married women, xiii
  in single women vs. single men, 174
Divorce(s)
  changing attitudes toward, 9
  marital counseling and, 28
  wife-initiated, 173, 174
    men's response to, 175–76
    missing responses to, 179–81
    reasons for, 176–77
    society's response to, 177–78, 181
Drama Kings
  assumptions of, about relationships,
    xii
  definition of, xi
  demands of, 27, 28–29
  negative traits of, xii, xvi, 188

  as portrayed in fiction, 15–16
  psyches of, 16–17
  relationships as viewed by, 30
  similarities between, 169–70
  strong women attracted to, xi–xii,
    16, 195–96
  types of (see Easygoing Guy; Feeling-
    Impaired Guy; Hit-and-Run
    Lover; Proprietor; Visitor)
  unchanging nature of, xiv, xv,
    xvi–xvii
  women's relationships with
    growth after, 170, 186, 193–95
    lessons learned from, xv–xvi, 170,
      185
    reasons for leaving, 30–31,
      173–74
    reasons for staying in, 171–73

E

Easygoing Guy (EGG)
  lessons learned from, 116–17
  myths about, 114
  story about, 97–111
  traits of, 97–98, 101, 102, 103, 104,
    108–11
    fantasizing about relationships,
      113
    laid-back manner, 97–98, 112
    privacy and mystery, 112–13
    reticence about sex, 99, 100, 113
    secret lives, 99, 113
    why women are taken in by, 114–16
    women's reaction to, 99, 100, 103–6
Education, of modern women, 12–13
Ehrenreich, Barbara, 13
Erikson, Erik, 193–94
Erotic Silence of the American Wife, The
  (Heyn), xiii

F

Feeling-Impaired Guy (FIG)
  lessons learned from, 168–69
  myths about, 167–68

stories about, 153–56, 157, 158–59, 160–63, 164–65
traits of, 153–54, 159, 163–64
  alternating moods, 155
  difficulty communicating, 157
  disinterest in others, 166–67
  inability to listen, 165
  lack of compassion, 162–63
  lack of emotional vitality, 166
  lack of feelings, 155–56, 159, 164–65, 166
  lack of guilt, 167
  nonattachment to others, 166, 168
  passivism, 157, 158
  perfectionism, 154
  spirituality, 159–60
why women are taken in by, 168
women's reaction to, 154, 155–56, 157, 158–59, 160–63, 164–65
Financial status, of modern women, 13
Fishman, Pamela M., 52–53

G
Gottman, John, 48–49, 190

H
Hit-and-Run Lover
  advice for victims of, 138
  lessons learned from, 150–51
  myths about, 148–50
  stories about, 119–28, 129–30, 131–38, 145–46, 148–49
    from man's point of view, 139–45
  traits of, 128–29, 130–31, 137–39
    aggression, 120, 121, 131, 146–47
    fantasizing, 125–26, 130, 146
    fight-or-flight response, 127–28, 133, 135–37, 139–40, 144
    persistence, 123–24, 131, 143, 147
    resentment of being counted on, 127, 133–34
  why women are taken in by, 150
  women's reaction to, 125, 126, 129–30, 131–32, 134, 136–37, 137–38, 146

I
Intimacy, 137, 187, 188, 191

J
Jealousy
  pathological
    abuse linked to, 85
    normal vs., 87–88

K
Kohut, Heinz, 193

L
Lifestyle choices, of modern women, 17–18

M
Mahler, Margaret, 193
Marriage
  idealization of, 178–79
  reasons for failure of, 175
  redefining relationships before, 190–91
  statistics on, 173–74
Marriage shock, xiii
Marriage Shock: The Transformation of Women into Wives (Heyn), xiii

N
Neurotic Styles (Shapiro), 73

P
Person, Ethel, 14
Pleasing
  vs. pleasure, women's conflict over, 14–15, 22–24
  as woman's role
    emergence of, 19–22
    rejection of, 196–97
Pleasure
  loss of, among women, xiii
  pleasing vs., women's conflict over, 14–15, 22–24
  power united with, 15
  women's desire for, 183–84
Power, pleasure united with, 15
Proprietor
  lessons learned from, 95
  myths about, 90–94
  response of male vs. female friends to, 89
  stories about, 63–72, 73–76, 77–78, 80–81, 82–83, 84–85, 85–87

Proprietor (cont.)
  traits of, 63
    aggression, 89
    attentiveness, 64–67
    attraction to strong women, 76–77
    controlling, 77–78
    hypersensitivity, 89
    jealousy, 74–76, 78–79, 87, 88, 90, 91–92
    paranoia, 72–73, 90–91
    persistence, 83
    possessiveness, 67–73
    rage, 69, 70, 71, 73–76, 79, 91
    sexual intensity, 64, 65
    use of sex to make up, 93–94
  why women are taken in by, 94
  women's reaction to, 65–67, 68, 69–71, 72, 74–75, 75–76, 78–79, 80–81, 82–83, 84–85, 85–86, 88

R
Real, Terrence, 192
Relational strength, 137, 191–93
Relationships
  with Drama Kings
    growth after, 170, 186, 193–95
    lessons learned from, xv–xvi, 170, 185
    reasons for leaving, 30–31, 173–74
    reasons for staying in, 171–73
  men's desires in, 188–89
  men's success in, 189–90
  redefining, before marriage, 190–91
  women's changing attitudes toward, 1–12, 14, 25–27, 30
  missing responses to, 179–81
  women's desires in, 171–72, 183–84, 187, 188, 191
  women's expectations of, 187
  women's sacrifices in, 184–85
Rescue fantasies, rejection of, 9–10

S
Shapiro, David, 73, 79
Steinem, Gloria, 9–10
Stosny, Steven, 90–91, 150–51
Strong women
  accomplishments of, 12–14
  attracted to Drama Kings, xi–xii, 16, 195–96

changing attitudes of, toward relationships, 1–12, 14, 25–27, 30
desires and needs of, 17, 54–55, 171–73
Drama Kings' demands of, 27, 28–29
emergence of, xiii–xv
learning from relationships with Drama Kings, xv–xvi
leaving Drama Kings, 30–31
profile of, 17, 29
relationship binds of, 29
traits of, xiv–xv
weaknesses of, 81

V
Visitor
  lessons learned from, 62
  married, 43, 60
  myth about, 60–61
  power of, 45, 51–52
  stories about, 33–43, 46–48, 51, 52, 54, 55–56
  traits of
    depression, 44
    fear of dating, 35, 39, 56–57
    fear of intimacy, 57–58
    helplessness in finding love, 58–59
    immovability, 49, 50–51
    inability to commit, 38–40, 42–43
    infidelity, 43–44
    lack of interest, 45, 51, 59–60
    loner, 43
    paranoia, 54–55
    sexual interest, 35, 40, 50, 56
    unavailability, 35, 36–37
vagueness through flattery, 58
  waiting game with, 49–50
  why women are taken in by, 61–62
women's reaction to, 34–35, 36–39, 40–43, 44–48, 49, 55–56, 61

W
Whitehead, Barbara Dafoe, 17
Winnicott, D. W., 1